Changing Society and the

Power

Robin Greenwood and
Hugh Burgess

First published in Great Britain in 2005

Society for Promoting Christian Knowledge
36 Causton Street
London SW1P 4ST

British Library Cataloguing-in-Publication Data
A catalogue record for this book is available from the British Library

ISBN 0-281-05684-6

10 9 8 7 6 5 4 3 2 1

Designed and typeset by Kenneth Burnley, Wirral, Cheshire
Printed in Great Britain by Ashford Colour Press

Contents

For Claire, Peter, Tim, Jo, Nyah and Katherine

And for Janet, Rosy, Rob and Sarah

Changing Society and the Churches

The social teaching of the churches from 1900 to 1970 came either from members of small radical Christian groups or else from the perspective of the established order of society. Today, neither approach will work. Small left-wing groups flourished in inner urban areas and provided support to the poor up to the 1970s. Much of Christian socialism was spread through groups that may have been small nationally but were of immense importance locally. Campaigning groups still exist but the crucial difference is that they generally do not have any religious commitment. They are instead quite secular bodies in which some members of faith communities are deeply involved.

Equally the middle axiom approach of the churches (where the accepted wisdom of social experts was put alongside the wisdom of leaders of the church) does not work either. The churches are too marginal to bring about this influence on society, although a few examples of this reasoning remain in the main denominations. But it is not a model for doing Christian social ethics overall any more. The alliance of secular wisdom and liberal theology has largely collapsed as well.

However, there is still an enormous need to change society, and the Church must be challenged to think about how this can be done. Hence the title of this series is Changing Society and the Churches. The series incorporates authors who can address this need. Their arguments might not necessarily come from any one political or religious viewpoint: this is not a left-wing or a right-wing series. Rather, it includes authors who can speak to the secular world using arguments that resonate in modern society, yet employ theological resources and the Christian heritage of spirituality to support their claims. It is equally important that these arguments are designed to change society and to get Christians involved.

Can such a thing be done? We would point to the example of Rowan Williams as an author who has long resonated with society and understands contemporary culture, and yet is not afraid to use examples from theology, spirituality and Christian engagement in society to back up his arguments. The result is a language that is neither 'churchy' nor secular and watered down. It is realistic about how marginal the churches are, but is not pessimistic. It speaks of the need for social change and is prepared to form alliances with non-Christian groups, but without denying the Christian basis of the argument.

The books in the series have a concrete reference and are aware that these issues demand action without offering facile solutions. They are books that explore new possibilities for society, whether from a right-wing or a left-wing position. All the books suggest why change is desirable and how it is possible.

The series is international in scope, although its concreteness may well draw on English examples, at least in the first books, since we wish authors to draw on their experience and our first authors are English. Later books may well argue from a viewpoint other than an English one. Increasingly both theology and the experience of Christians can no longer be confined to one country, and the challenges of the twenty-first century are expressed across different cultures and societies. That may well mean offering a different understanding of the relationship of society and Church for the British situation. Even so, it is important that wherever the author comes from there is an engagement with secular society using the resources of Christian tradition and theology. The aim is to bring about social change and church involvement.

Al McFadyen
Department of Theology and Religious Studies, University of Leeds

Peter Sedgwick
Board for Social Responsibility, Church of England

Foreword

by the Most Reverend Dr Barry C. Morgan, Archbishop of Wales

When the phrase 'theological' is used in modern society, it is often meant pejoratively – the viewpoint advanced is seen as being arcane and irrelevant. The argument of this book, however, is that if we get our theology right (words about and understanding of God) then this will help, not hinder, how we view our society and indeed our world. It is precisely because we often have a distorted or false way of seeing God that our understanding of so much else goes awry. Thus if God is seen in terms of omnipotence, power and strength, regulating the world at whim, that will be reflected in the way we deal with one another in authoritarian, dominating ways. These chapters help us to explore and reshape our analogies for God so that embodied Christian practice can make a significant contribution to human interpersonal and corporate relationships.

The book is therefore a challenge not just to governments, business organizations and human relations, but particularly to the Church of God which claims to follow Jesus but often fails to live by the message in which it purports to believe. Those of us who exercise any kind of leadership will find this book an uncomfortable read since it challenges the way we so often exercise authority and power. It is full of insights from the Bible, the Christian tradition and the worlds of business and organizational management.

At its heart is its understanding of God not as monad but as Trinity – 'a community of relational difference'. What Robin Greenwood and Hugh Burgess offer us here is an interdisciplinary reflection on how our fulfilment as human beings can only be found in our relationship to that trinitarian God. In turn this shapes the way we relate to and respect others as unique and valuable persons.

Preface

I extend deep appreciation and gratitude to many who have in different ways contributed to the writing of this book. Among the list of those whose conversations in recent years have inspired and encouraged me, I want to mention especially Ken Bennett, Adrian Berry, Ken Booth, Stephen Brown, Patrick Coleman, Jenny Dawson, Norman Doe, Judith Gregory, Richard Hill, Margaret and Chris Honoré, Phil Kirk, Conny Matera-Rogers, Paul Maybury, Manon Parry, Caroline Pascoe, Robert Paterson, Alan Payne, Philip Richardson, Chris Samuel, Malcolm Squires and Anthony Stone. I also thank the Archbishop and Bishops of the Church in Wales for their support and expectation that an integral part of my work as Ministry Officer has been to research and contribute to the international and ecumenical debate about the character and task of the Church. I owe a continuing debt of gratitude to Daniel W. Hardy, who has taught me so much about possibilities for the future of the Church. Above all I thank my wife Claire, whose theological, spiritual and psychological perspectives on the Church's potential role in society are a rich resource and creative challenge to me.

Robin

I would first of all like to thank Robin for inviting me to collaborate with him in the writing of this book, for his enthusiasm and unfailing support in what has been an illuminating and challenging experience. Also to those many Christian people who have, over many years and in many places supported and guided me, often without being aware of their impact, I extend my warmest thanks and appreciation, but most notably to Ian Findlay, Andrew and Narelle Gatenby, Ken and Jessica Gordon, Valerie Jones, Chris and Jenny Potter and Roger and Christina Pullen, and all my friends in the Cursillo Movement who continue to provide warm support and encouragement. But alongside those who have supported me in my Christian life I also acknowledge a deep debt of gratitude to Jack

Beeson, Phil Honor, Peter O'Keefe and Eric Stanley, each of whom at different times saw something in me that I could not see in myself, and who allowed me space to make mistakes and to discover the deep excitement of work. But my deepest thanks, appreciation and admiration go to my wife Janet and my children Rosy, Robert and Sarah, who have supported me and uncomplainingly accepted my disappearance into the study over many months.

Hugh

We jointly wish to thank our editors Ruth McCurry, Alistair McFadyen and Peter Sedgwick, and also Heather Jenkins for her administrative efficiency and encouragement.

Introduction

The self-generating power of God courses through the veins of every living thing. For those of the baptized who give themselves to be formed by the life of Jesus Christ, there is the restless invitation to grow over a lifetime. Open to the energy of the triune God, the corporate and always destabilizing performance of loving relation, we anticipate in our whole being the new creation that is God's passionate purpose. We invite the reader to engage in an exchange about a divinely inspired notion and experience of power, through which three persistent strands are interwoven.

- First that, with both discretion and humility, the mainline churches have much to learn, from public discourse and from contemporary and historical insights into organizational theory and practice, about the distribution and effective working of power.
- Second that, through reflection on and within its own tradition, the Church critiques and contributes to the restoration of society. Its task is to reformulate language and imaginative practices that contribute to the reconfiguring of human identity and the sustaining of all forms of purposeful organization and local human community.
- Third that churches, as communities of distinctive character (yet acknowledging their problematic and flawed practice), have the competence to counter all that debilitates and to show to the world vital clues for re-visioning all living.

'Power' features prominently in everyday life and language. A trawl of the day's newspapers reveals that those seeking to carry out reforms, to impose sanctions, to arrest potential terrorists, to send manned flights safely into space, to maintain a strong economy, to counter deaths from hunger-related diseases, to win superiority through armed conflict, to achieve maximum capacity in national economy and government, are determined to stay 'in power'. Power is a pivotal concept with myriad associations and definitions, a concept that includes a spectrum of notions shaping human identity and relationships, and yet in everyday practice 'power' is often associated solely with ideas of domination, authority, control, hierarchy or other similar definitions. That power is so immediately recognized in this way reflects our view of the world, dominated by great powers, global enterprise, trans-national corporations and many unseen or unrecognized forces, and with our lives apparently controlled increasingly by national government or the European Union (EU). But for Christians, notions of power go far beyond this, touching gentler, mutual, holistic and inclusive ideas that recognize and celebrate the contributions of the apparently powerless: power understood as the energy that invigorates, restores, renews and makes it possible for the powerless to have a voice and to achieve great things even in the face of huge challenges. We also understand power to encompass ideas of capability and capacity: 'I have the power to read or to understand, or to make complex decisions based on application of previously acquired knowledge and skills.' In a very real sense, power restricted solely to control is severely limiting, as it seeks to dominate others and thus denies or constrains their voice, and the application of their capability and capacity into a particular direction. We therefore argue for a renewed understanding of power and, flowing from this, transfigured ways of dealing one with another.

The goal of this book is to reconsider how power may be exercised in order to renew and repair both Church and society by holding a trans-disciplinary conversation on theories and practices of power. As well as showing that the Church has much to learn through interaction with society, we also assert that the Church should not be afraid to retrieve from its own tradition insights into the nature and practice of power that can contribute distinctively to the world's re-creation. Throughout the book we offer illustrations, drawn from our personal experience in the Church and in business, which bring into sharp focus the wider issues examined.

As we draw on renewed explorations of biblical imagery, and the reappraisal of a trinitarian experience and understanding of the power that God vests in each person and community, the reader is invited to recognize in themselves and all the personal and organizational networks to which they contribute, the need to move beyond inherited notions of power as domination and polarization. Through a combination of allowing the Christian narrative to shape the practices of the Church and developing prophetic leadership, the energy, capability and capacity of individuals and groups may be released, empowering them in new ways to serve God's loving purpose for creation. God's truth is known and practised through passionate, committed and corporate discipleship. Churches practise the meaning they find in the trinitarian God for the life of the world.

Our intention is to offer a compelling resource for disciples in all walks of life, lay as well as clergy, bishops and others, who are helping to reframe and energize daily engagement with people, organizations and churches in the light of the Church's corporate faith in the trinitarian God of love. The common vocation of Christians is to accompany and love the world into responding to God. Part of the task of loving is persistently to show what the other cannot or will not see, in the name of justice, righteousness, freedom, genuine mutuality and un-doing all that exploits.

We share a conviction that power is understood most truly when interactive, widely distributed and available for the common good of all. However, in our own experience, we are coming to recognize that life runs better when we have the honesty to own up to our own 'shadow' side. There is part of all of us, apparently kept hidden, that is not about love or altruism. In a cluster of motives, there is a straightforward desire in each of us for power over others, to have our ideas adopted, to make our lives more comfortable – whatever the cost to others. Like the mother of the sons of thunder, part of us wants our children to be the ones who sit on the right and the left. The world's violence, politics, starvation, business, communities and churches are filled with this confusing mixture of rivalry and mutual care. Knowing this struggle in others and ourselves has to be a strong element of any honest way of talking about and planning for society and the world. It is tough work when we dare to confront and own up to our naked, Machiavellian desire to be in the limelight, to be 'top', 'in charge', and triumphant. Dread of our own daring is countered in the oft-quoted words of Marianne Williamson that 'Our deepest fear is not that we are inadequate. Our deepest fear is that we are powerful beyond measure' (Williamson, 1992, ch. 7).

1 | Authority

Why authority?

What is allowed? Christianity is frequently lampooned for supposedly offering a mere list of prohibitions rather than freedom in Christ. The current debate within Anglicanism on the authority of scripture, on the right of churches throughout the world to make their own decisions, and on homosexual relations, highlights the need for a rigorous consideration of issues of authority. The lives of people, families, churches and organizations are embodied in their continuing, dynamic relationship with language, texts, narratives, particular historical figures, models and events. As we explore in this chapter, the achievement of any goal, or the development of particular forms of communal living, implies bringing underlying views of authority into our consciousness. For those formed within Christian tradition, as well as living within the complexities of the modern world, the invitation is offered to grow consciously as human beings in response to the call of a loving and demanding God. To be a community characterized by the love of God, commanded to work for the coming of God's reign, what particular authority is required?

This study on power begins with an exploration of authority, not as a given, imposed and implacable command, but as arising from the truth to be learned through engagement with the dynamic life of God, the Trinity. Our proposal is that authority from a Christian perspective is not to be found in fixed formulae and immutable descriptions of the state of the world. It is more likely to be discovered through risky and freely chosen interdisciplinary openness to the trinitarian God. This is the authority we find today, interwoven within networks, fields and processes: enacted by children, young people, parents and teachers; natural to many ethnic groups throughout the world; and explored increasingly by the baptized laity and clergy within the churches of every age and our own. In every field, whether of business, music, education, health, ecology or natural sciences, the adventure of finding mature humanity requires a fluid basis that is neither narrowly constrained nor boundlessly free. Instead a generous, self-limiting, mutual awareness may provide momentum and initial clues for authoritative personhood and sociality, grounded in the ultimate authority of God.

Authentic Christian community

Critiquing structures and theories of power (in ourselves, institutions, images and ideologies) is a compelling concern of ethical Christian community living. A vital but difficult starting point is that, at every point in human life together, the potential exists for us to be recipients or perpetrators of violence, domination and exploitation. However, profound hope lies in our choice to belong to and live fully as the community of the baptized people of God, called to demonstrate and proclaim the unique hope for the world arising from Jesus Christ, crucified, risen and ascended.

In the New Testament, opposing the principalities and powers was regarded as more than an interhuman struggle. Under diverse names, hardly connecting with life today, these forces appear in all four Gospels, along with 1 Thessalonians, as well as Colossians, Ephesians and 2 Peter. The Church is the group of those who recognize their share in the Resurrection victory of Christ, with the responsibility for taking their place in the eschatological drama, the final battle for the reign of God, through unmasking exaggerated importance or pretended harmlessness and in living the 'message of peace in word and deed' (Schlier, 1961, p. 59). Although Bultmann, in the mid twentieth century, demonstrated that we no longer live in the small world-view of the first century AD, Marva Dawn warns against the Church fighting for justice in merely human terms (Dawn, 2001). The particular identity of Christian community is rooted in faith that expects the God who promises and yearns for *shalom*, indeed to act to unmask pretence and restore all that is broken. Supported by Israel's core testimony that Yahweh judges and acts for justice, the Church, although offering hospitality to and wrestling with many human endeavours, knows its unique contribution, as expecting the God of impossibilities to continue to work wonders. A crucial rider to this is that the Church, recalling its own propensity for self-idolatry, will seek the antidotes of humility, self-reflection, repentance, and embrace only of the true power, known in weakness. Although Jesus in his body was savaged and his own power disregarded, he gives authority to the Church, through the Spirit, to know and to work out and realize God's truth about the dynamics of undistorted power. History shows the ways in which the Church, as the supposed bearer of the Good News of Jesus, has developed ideas of God that have legitimized distorted practices of power (Spalding, 2001, p. 57). Yet this same Church, under-girded by the God who never lets go, is in fact a bridge between the many disciplines of those contributing to the repair of the world and its people, so as to enable them to come to their promised good end.

While respecting diverse insights into organizational and personal relating, uniquely the Church has the joyful gift and responsibility to demonstrate the full potential of life together in close relationships, families, neighbourhoods, nations and the world. This companionship model is built around mutual participation, not hierarchy. With humility and recognition of its own failing, this task includes the critiquing and re-visioning of dominant patterns of human behaviour. Recognizing how far we fall short in the practice of relating, we (Hugh and Robin) have only dared to attempt this book because of the resources offered by Christian spirituality and theology and the gifts that emerge through sharing in the eucharistic life of the baptized and baptizing community. Opposing hopelessness and nurturing the moral environment is an integral element of the fidelity of the communities called, formed and gathered around Jesus; loyal to him, exemplars of his vision, and called and blessed through the Spirit of God, they thus underwrite the importance of the contribution of all people in the everyday. These messianic communities, endowed with the same energetic Spirit that rested on Jesus, are sent to proclaim God's reign as the power of unconditional grace to make persons, relationships and bodies whole. To practise dynamic Christian community is to expect the trinitarian God to be innovative in drawing us to be gripped and involved in working out new possibilities for social order, politics, ecology, economics and personal relating. In this sense the practice of economics is essentially about justice, and therefore its language and assumptions are a key area for Christian debate and discipline, internationally and locally. In the light of the Lambeth Commission on Communion (The Windsor Report, 2004), Archbishop Njongonkulu Ndungane of South Africa looks to the Church to show the world how to disagree 'within a relationship of interdependence, a living example of autonomy-in-communion' (*Church Times*, 22 October 2004, p. 10).

The prayerful, thoughtful intervention of the Church of Jesus, the community who know and live the meaning of power in relation when intimately rooted in the life of Christ, is desperately needed in a world of injustice, fear and isolation. Both Luke and John believed passionately that the emergence of the Church was bound up with Christ's sending the Spirit who anointed the disciples to continue the mission of Jesus. The Church is the continuation of the work of Christ as anointed by the Spirit to fulfil the Father's will. The task of the Church is to become the fruit of Christ's work and an early sign of God's reign, constantly re-finding itself through being a people gathered in the Spirit to worship the one God. The Church's practice of *koinonia* (communion, community and communication) is catholic, not merely a collection of individuals or of separated churches, because the Spirit creates and anoints the community to continue Christ's work of transforming all humanity into a single people of God. God is the ultimate communion of Persons in friendship. In God 'we live and move and have our being' (Acts 17.28). By opening each person and community to every other person and community, and all of them to God's universal eschatological reign, the Spirit makes the Church into a community determined by its reconciled and mutually enriching diversity (Acts 2), an organic whole with many functions. The Church's authority, when vulnerable, God-shaped and sustained, is therefore open to being a continuation within the fabric of human society of the process iconically represented by the Spirit anointing Jesus in the Jordan.

The Christian tradition bears witness to a long theological wrestling with the question of authority. Christianity arose as a young reform movement within Judaism, reassessing the authority of law, temple, land and family in the light of a fresh understanding of God's work in the world. Every human being has the potential for personal relationship with God and the concomitant invitation to participate in the project Jesus names as 'the Kingdom of God'. Despite the exclusion of Jesus by the religious leaders of his day, leading inexorably to his crucifixion outside the city wall, a radically transformed understanding of religious authority was born through his life, death and resurrection. Current disputes in the Anglican Communion are part of the chain of dilemmas, both creative and divisive, within Christian history relating to the authority of scripture, leaders, the Church and the individual disciple. Successive generations play their part in thinking, praying and exploring how to be most faithful to the tradition, making what later generations judge to be either gross errors (crusades and support of apartheid) or enlightened steps forward (opposition to slavery, development of free education and campaigns for prison reform). The 'handing over' of Jesus to others contains elements of both inspiration and betrayal.

There are three authoritative dimensions to a eucharistic church that lives by praising God or giving thanks. These are: proclaiming the Good News of God's presence in the universe and in every human journey, celebrating God's gift of life, and practising the new life in Christ characterized by some form of dying to self. In the eucharist these three dimensions interconnect, the identity of the Church being celebrated and critiqued as a society deliberately egalitarian in structure. Those who define themselves as 'the norm' while relativizing those who are 'different' or 'other', fail to give glory to the God who is the defining community of difference in unity. This God is the sole fount of authority in Christian community. Sociologically, hierarchies may be tolerated for the structured and effective management of work and to avoid confusion. However, if God, as revealed in Jesus through the Spirit, is the ultimate symbol of authority, there can be no acceptance of a hierarchical principle in which one group or individual may pretend to enduring patterns of predominance.

There is no need here to recapitulate the history of the Church's experiments with different patterns of authority and organization of the Christian community, whether Roman, Celtic, Orthodox, medieval, reformed or enlightened. These have been exhaustively documented and critiqued by others and continue to influence contemporary exploration and analysis of the ordering of Christian identity (see, for example, Schillebeeckx, 1980; Gunton and Hardy, 1989; Sedgwick in Ford and Stamps, 1996).

Issues that pervade the contemporary debate critically include the authority of scripture; the authority of the Church in relation to the individual Christian, bishops and clergy and laity; the authority of laity in a 'collaborative' church; the institution as opposed to the intimate community, the wider Church and the local; and questions as to the essence of the practice of *communio*. The period since Vatican II, with its afterburn of writing, the publication of the Lima texts on Baptism, Eucharist and Ministry, and the massive ecumenical debate of recent decades, has unmasked many forms of domination – of women, of lay people, of clergy in hierarchies, and of all whose intelligence is at variance with inherited linear patterns. Although anxious fundamentalisms of many forms resist the move toward authentic, courteous, difference-embracing patterns of church organization and debate, the perspective of this study is that the struggle to discover Trinity-inspired forms of authority is vital for human living in the unfolding cosmos. In searching for the criteria of true Christian community, we are participating both in God's future and in the process of transforming the world in response to God.

The determination to obliterate people's identities and the constant stream of tragedies of ethnic cleansing or of children undernourished, taken as prostitutes, soldiers or suicide bombers, constantly challenges the authenticity of churches that fail to be active in a world of the oppressed. Authority, asserted as self-legitimated violence against the person, cries out for a response from those who believe that humanity, authentically understood, is a practice of graced sociality that deliberately sets out to echo the relation to each other of the persons of the Trinity (McFadyen, 2000, p. 200). Embodied faith in Jesus is about life in all its fullness for everyone. It has no place for different degrees of participation, for specially privileged initiates and for banishing some from the circle of power.

Community living, if preoccupied with itself, fails to contribute distinctively to the context in which it is set, ignoring its task of promoting the mutual relation between human living and creation. God's mission, the Church's work, lies in challenging and helping to deconstruct patterns of society that are formed in terms of endless false dichotomies. This mission can be frustrated when churchgoers and citizens, enjoying relatively predictable lives in the West, fail to probe what hinders and to contribute to the recreating of common life. Essentially churches have a vocation determinedly to consider and work out in practice the implications for open and interconnected human identity in every exercise of authority, not least that of critiquing the circumstances and demands of their own living.

Who is our God?

A passage from Martin Luther King Jr's letter from jail in Birmingham, Alabama invites us to confess faith in God and to inhabit the consequences:

> I have travelled the length and breadth of Alabama, Mississippi and all the other Southern states. On sweltering summer days and crisp autumn mornings I have looked at her beautiful churches with their spires pointing heavenward. I have beheld the impressive outlay of her massive religious education buildings. Over and over I have found myself asking, Who worships here? Who is their God? (quoted by Jinkins, 1999, p. 85)

The Holy Spirit renews Christian theology every day in response to unfolding, complex events: our recognition, interpretation and applied understanding of God at work in creation daily mediates our behaviour. Recent research into the ministries of some of the moderates critically addressed by King, indicates how his influence was often more subtle and less adversarial than has been supposed (Miller, 2004, p. 157). God constantly gives Christian communities and disciples new chances to repent, to move on contingently but with God's constant gift, to exercise authority as reassessed by Jesus and as a sign of the profound friendship that characterizes the Kingdom of God.

However, it must be with great caution that we dare to rehearse the words added in later centuries to those of Jesus to the disciples in response to their request to be taught how to pray, 'For yours is the Kingdom, the Power and the Glory'. Notions of God's power evolve in every time and place according to our insight, need and situation. Significant questions must include: who is the Holy Mystery we dare to call God? Who is Jesus that we worship and proclaim, represented by the absurd emblem of the cross? Who is this Spirit who comes to comfort and lead this broken world? Often when we are faced with the experience of deep darkness, God can seem terrifyingly absent and speech about God incomprehensible (Acts 17.29; 1 Timothy 6.16; John 1.18; Romans 11.33–4; 1 Corinthians 13.9, 12).

The Catholic theologian Elizabeth Johnson, notably, has related the sufferings of the world to the mystery of God as Wisdom

(Sophia) whose attributes are mutual relation, radical equality, and community in diversity, threefold *koinonia* (Johnson, 1998). She stands among those who have challenged the notion of singleness in God through a redevelopment of the ancient Greek theological term *perichoresis* to signify the interpersonal dynamic, the being-in-one-another, permeation without confusion of the Trinity. In contrast to the all-powerful and unilateral God who legitimizes the world-view often known as theism, and its concomitant patterns of authority, Johnson retrieves a notion of God's relational power. Such power, she says, offers a liberating strength which sustains mutual, loving relationship through the freedom to become vulnerable.

To a world of anguish, familiar with pain, Christian and Jewish faith speaks consistently of God who, though hidden, is always drawing near, who is the companion on the dark road of suffering, and who acts to make a difference. A significant dilemma is the impotence that results from the Church's practical and linguistic collusion with inherited perspectives about God's monarchical or patriarchal power, perspectives that seem to have little connection with the Jesus of the Gospels or the earliest, Spirit-led, radical experiments in corporate discipleship. For centuries, classically formed Christian theology taught belief in the unilateral power of God as transcendent, impassive, immutable, patriarchal, unchanging, self-sufficient, and absolutely beyond humanity.

Despite the contemporary demise of theism in north-western Europe and the recovery and development of relational speech about God, the legacy of monarchy is still pervasive. Once considered the divinely ordered means of grace, a hierarchical church structure is now exposed as severely restricting its intellectual and emotional authority in discourse about coherent futures for society.

A sharp result of this inheritance is the prevalent male-dominated status of clergy as virtuosos, demanding passive submission. Within both communities and individuals, great persistence is required to uproot such long-established disfigurements of Christian ministerial practice. For example, throughout the UK, despite the rehabilitation of a social trinitarian key to all theology and the rhetoric of 'shared ministry', the balance of policy-making in the Anglican and Roman Catholic churches lies with bishops. Although bishops and other senior figures habitually deny their power, they often contribute to a culture of hierarchical secrecy with a consequent low expectation of the 'rank and file'. This culture frequently disables plans to develop 'collaborative patterns of ministry' as well as breeding resentment and infantile behaviour. In contrast, when power is acknowledged as deeply relational and open, individuals and councils are free to use it creatively, even joyfully. However, experience testifies that the raising of disagreements and encouragement of creative conflict can still be equated with disloyalty and unreliability.

The exercise of authority merely as controlling power usually points to an absence of a vibrant understanding of the work of the Holy Spirit and to an over-simplistic linkage of Christology to the male person of Jesus, ignoring the pre-existent and eschatological Christ of the Trinity. The practice of Christian authority is diminished when it is forgotten that the witness and interpretation of the Holy Spirit is seminal to opening up fresh possibilities for the work of Christ in ever new situations. The writings of Paul show the Holy Spirit drawing the world to its final purposes in Christ. For example, the Spirit bears witness with our spirit that we are no longer bound but God's children (Romans 8.14–17; Galatians 4.6–7), sharing in the tension between the suffering and glory of Christ's own life. The work of the Spirit in the Church is also to hold in good relation the more 'charismatic' and the practical (kindness and self-control) so that life in the Spirit is a rich mixture of the ordinary and extraordinary (1 Corinthians 12.28–30; Galatians 5.22–3).

For John the Holy Spirit brings forgiveness, judgement and truth through the witness of Christ's real presence. The work of the Spirit is to show to the Church the vibrant 'abba' relationship between Jesus and the Father, not merely in the life of Jesus of Nazareth but in the glorified, risen life of Christ (Williams, 2000, ch. 8). Enacting that relationship in Christian community now, through the agency of the Spirit, enables the Church to demonstrate something of the liberating and transforming authority of Christian faith.

We need therefore an end to those dualistic assumptions in classical Christian theology that have contributed to commonly accepted, dominant paradigms of power and to the restrictive shaping of human life into apparent opposites: male/female, black/white, gay/straight, able-bodied/disabled, the cosmos/humanity. A hierarchical understanding of God, as the remote pinnacle of transcendence, envisions a world of relationships in which a minority of the dominant are considered to have power over the people below them and they in turn have power over those below them, so descending to the most alienated ones at the bottom of the pile,

'God, angels, saints, man, woman, planet and in addition to dualisms of black/white, straight/gay, and so on; the list is endless' (Isherwood, 2004, p. 141). Dualistic, hierarchical notions of authority are competitive or adversarial. So authority is regarded as being possessed by individuals, with the implication that others do not possess it. People at the top decide: people at the bottom execute.

The hymn line, 'The rich man in his castle, the poor man at his gate', is sung only infrequently today, but it remains as a lingering trace of how notions of God, authority and market forces interweave in every sphere of institutional and co-operative life. Naïve understandings of imperialism, that emasculate the dignity and ignore the feelings of those labelled as inferior, provide further examples of paradigms of power woven from particular forms of Christian thought and action. This distorted theology of authority continues to divide the world and has led to millions of people suffering abuse, rape and genocide, often in the name of Christ. As the Church's inherited public credibility diminishes, it appears to have lost its sense of the nature of God's friendship and love and therefore its essential reason for being. The challenge is to wake up, believe in the reality of God's relational presence in every situation and so be reformed, recalling the authority truly given to followers in every age by Christ (Matthew 28.18), the servant leader and revealer of God as communion of love. Instead of drowsy self-pity, the Church must risk a greater degree of self-criticism and representation of Jesus-shaped patterns of authoritative faith practice.

Life after death?

Christianity has to a large degree formed the world of social and personal relations in which issues of authority are played out. The contemporary fabric of the world is in desperate need of rescue from exclusivity and narrowness. This requires the Church to rediscover itself in order to contribute urgently, but with humility, from the well of its unique tradition and in discourse with many others, to a wider rediscovery of what it means to be human in God's creation. Christian communities, as neither self-contained nor self-sufficient (and in all their confused arguments about the meaning of discipleship), must engage imaginatively with anyone who is willing, in order to contribute to the retexturing of social and global relations.

Yet instead we find a Church preoccupied with self-maintenance and spiralling out of connection with Western culture and society. There is a growing literature of statistics on institutional decline and on methods that might reverse the churches' fortunes (Jackson, 2002). Children's evangelism, courses for seekers, and cell church (Booker and Ireland, 2003) are important but they fail to engage with deeper questions about the disengagement of European culture from the meanings Christians find in God. Certainly, through niche marketing, concentrating on a single focus, some churches buck the trend in terms of adherence. But generally, while churches strain to keep going a bit longer, these questions are not faced: why pour immense human and financial resources into this way of being the Church at all? how does the worship and activity of church connect with the messy, confused lives of those whose stories fill the newspapers each day?

Fresh expressions of church must be less about how to keep traditional churches open and growing and more about how this 'doing of church' at all contributes to God's purposes in an infinite number of situations. While European churches have continued, at worst, to perpetuate belief in a petulant, monarchical and impassive deity, and at best passively to condone this view, governments and the general public have largely pushed belief and its implications to the edge of the arena of authoritative decision-making. Curiously though, while secular universities query why public money should be squandered on thinking about 'God' at all, public health authorities increasingly regard the deployment of chaplains (of various faiths) as a vital ingredient in the overall healing process.

A marginalized Church lives on the knife-edge of either becoming preoccupied with its own survival or becoming an alluring ghetto for those exuberantly converted to a homogeneous creed, or with a preference for hearing strident voices from the far distant past. Generally speaking, traditional or institutional churches with ponderous inherited structures and listed buildings are experiencing inexorable meltdown, whilst pentecostalist churches experience exponential growth. Robin Gill's research identifies the successful growth of small-scale sects or new religious movements that have a strong tendency towards exclusivity and sectarianism. Currently in the Western world such churches are in the ascendant at the expense of consciously inclusive denominations (Gill, 2003, p. 217). Gill tempers this conclusion with the additional proposal that the strong-minded individuals typically recruited to such churches tend, after initially finding reassurance, to be excluded or to exclude themselves when differences of opinion arise.

Whether Western European and North American Christianity has a vital future, and in what forms, receives a high level of academic theological and sociological attention (Davie, 2004). In the traditional mainline churches, underlying anxiety about clergy conditions of service, planned reductions in the numbers of stipended ministers and strategies for 'organizational re-engineering' (Barrow, 2003, p. 11) all contribute to a picture in which churches are facing the death of their current incarnation. Throughout the UK chapels, along with post offices, pubs, libraries, schools and shops, go by the wall, possibly after belated bursts of local protest.

A late twentieth-century assumption, widespread among Christians, was that the Church, in itself, was unimportant and indeed was only too often implicated in, or silent in the face of, the world's tragedies. 'You don't have to go to church to be a Christian', the unofficial slogan of a confident, financially independent Church, remains a prevalent view. A recent statistical article in *The Times* was headed 'We believe in Easter; but not in going to church' (10 April 2004). The renewal of theology and practice engendered by the Second Vatican Council caused an explosion of hope concerning the vocation of laity in society and of the Church as witness for the gospel in the world. In the post Second World War era, Anglican bishops John Robinson and Joost de Blank were prominent leaders in a movement to challenge malaise through recalling the Church to its vocation as the Body of Christ, identified, learned and expressed through the parish communion (McBrien, 1966). Exhilarating liturgy, open house groups, burgeoning congregations and a desire to link faith with ordinary living were characteristics of this movement, summed up in the offertory procession. As lay people carefully brought the elements of bread, wine and water, together with the collection plate, to the priest at the altar, they were an embodiment of the contemporary slogan, 'The Mass is the centre of our lives'. The potential of the corporate authority of the Church in all its people scattered in the world remains huge, despite the accidents of historical institutions. In the UK, the Parish and People Movement, encapsulated in the vivid ministry of Ernie Southcott at St Wilfrid's, Halton in Leeds, was a radical turning point in the embracing of risky and often messy incarnation in which everyone counted.

Repenting of, and giving up false status and the holding of power over others is a vital but elusive key to developing and proudly exposing to society the practice of the Good News. Every new generation needs its prophetic pilot projects as we search for the next step. The work of bishops, other church leaders and their colleagues is to foster and clear a space for such possibilities, often through muddle and conflict. Churches that are unconcerned about defining their powerbase are dangerous and can be threatening. Theology, in a variety of ways (liberation theology, feminist and womanist theologies, and engagement with the changes in world-view sometimes called 'late' or 'post' modern), is contributing to a reappraisal of the Church's nature and role in society. As the embodiment of Christ and the way in which he continues God's work in the world, the Church loses its energy when it becomes preoccupied with its own shortcomings and internal problems. Rather the Church is summoned constantly to commit itself to rediscovering its purpose and shape for each new situation and, in the process, constantly relearning its own character. The relatively wealthy Church of several decades ago could complacently adopt a near horizontal attitude to its own authority and effectiveness in society, citing freedom of religion and adopting a liberal universalism that blamed public fecklessness for failing to come to worship. 'Implicit religion', in which church statements skirt round offending society by avoiding the mention of God, assumes inherited money in the bank and inhibits rather than empowers God's people. Furthermore, the communitarian critique of liberalism (notably by Alasdair MacIntyre and Stanley Hauerwas) jettisons the notion of the free, rational individual and the person of faith who is not profoundly formed by communities of tradition and ethical discourse.

The ubiquitous brown road-sign points to the current development of cheerful church tourist trails, instrumental in attracting new funds for the upkeep of church buildings. The danger is that churches become museums through partnership with nostalgia and heritage agencies. Their success, some even becoming involved with the national curriculum, can be seen as an oblique way of witnessing to the unchurched and as a healthy contribution to the building up of lattices of neighbourhood. The question is: how can this be integrated with the development of growing and joyfully authoritative church communities that more directly challenge us to allow God's love to flood our hearts and lives?

A casual observer of visitors to heritage centres might gain the impression that nostalgia very well suits the needs of the moderately healthy, wealthy and successful, but God's movement of love to the pain of the world requires more than this. Rich experience recognizes that lively and outward-looking church community is fostered when buildings can be used flexibly and more creatively through art, drama, poetry, pastoral care and many forms of liturgy, prayer and learning. Churches abdicate authority if the buildings that represent such a massive proportion of their resources actually disable them from serving those in critical physical and emotional need, expecting nothing in return. But when churches become almost exclusively fossilized heritage sites, they lose their true definition.

As recent experiments in church development show, models of church that deliberately promote the notion that there are many ways of belonging and commitment are likely to carry more weight and be more attractive than those that write off as 'fringe' all those who seek faith outside a dominant form of practice, such as attendance at the Sunday morning eucharist. For example, current explorations of 'parallel church' provide ways for developing radically different spiritual journeys for different groups of people, respecting that the Holy Spirit works uniquely with each one. Instead of being regarded as a problem, those who do not attend the Sunday eucharist are recognized as needing parallel and equal but different provision. Schemes to meet this need have been carried out and are currently being discussed. For example, in one parish with a building of cathedral-like proportions and in dire need of repair, the worshipping congregation is exploring a mission strategy which includes the possibility of basing a residential community at the church and developing the church as a multi-purpose building to include a café and a suitable, comfortable worship space. Rooted in regular prayer in the church throughout each day, energy is being released for a number of ministries among parents and children, schools, community groups and the elderly, as well as alternative forms of worship with others in the neighbourhood. The ambitious plan of this faith community, focused on 'round the clock prayer', includes the provision of safe open outdoor space, an eating place, accommodation, learning resources, creative art work, silent space, worship, and mentors and listeners.

Similar stories can be found across the UK, usually depending on both the entrepreneurial personality of the leader and on a falling in love with God by many members of the church. A faith that lets go of security allows a radically new possibility with long-term implications. There is a desperate need for churches who believe that with God all things are possible and that God's love includes even those, or particularly those, who find Sunday morning worship inaccessible and excluding. Sociological and statistical observations of religious trends, and predictions of the irreversible demise of Christian knowledge, faith and institutions (Bruce, 2003, pp. 53–63) make a vital contribution. But they need to be in dialogue with other disciplines (scriptural, theological, pastoral, liturgical and spiritual) as they are based on a limited understanding of people or local communities. Is it even possible simply to be an observer of religious practice? Can a faith community be understood or interpreted by one who does not surrender to the profound rhythm and movement of faith?

The world needs Christian community: clergy and people who will sacrifice their time, dignity, energy, security and freedom in the unique practice of community that follows Christ's example to live in a loving and dangerous liaison with the complex surrounding cultures. Each Christian has a contribution to offer towards making dynamic connection between their personal belief, their community of faith and ordinary encounters with individuals and groups. Society teems with those in their thirties and forties who, having lost much of their youthful optimism that things would somehow turn out, and at the end of their human resource, are just a breath away from receiving the love and challenge of Jesus Christ through the Spirit. The testing question is whether we and our churches have sufficient faith and expectation to see this and make time to respond in a mixture of sensitivity and confidence. Lysanne Sizoo reports how in secularized Sweden a 'monastery' has been established within Kumla prison. Some forty inmates have been enabled to build up confidence and to begin the journey of seeing their lives from a renewed perspective, through making Ignatian retreats (Sizoo, 2004). If the world belongs to and is enthreaded with God, our calling is to be witnesses that God breaks out still.

Can we talk?

Is there sufficient basis for conversation now between 'secular' society and communities of Christian faith, practical theology and the human sciences? Churches have a chequered history in their practice and imagery of the distribution of power and authority. Critically, research has documented the high incidence of Christians, with the profoundest of religious convictions, who fail to avoid the culture of power-grabbing and the linking of self-worth with achievement (Childs, 1995, p. 23). Popular speech about God, inside as well as beyond the Church, is frequently linked with the dominating and dualistic language of previous centuries. On the surface at least, for most people in the West today, God appears to be irrelevant and Christianity a spent force. This view is compounded when the Church fails in its credibility as an effective challenge to all that dominates and diminishes through the despising and torturing of God incarnate (Mantin, 2004, p. 212).

The complicity of institutional Christianity with imperial and hierarchical behaviour has frequently made damaging contributions to patterns of disempowerment rather than emancipation. A Western visitor to Russia, talking to an Orthodox priest soon after the fall of Marxist socialism, remarked on the welcome news that the Church, instead of being repressed, was again included in the infrastructure of society. When the priest was asked why he thought this was now possible, he replied, 'Because the people have short memories'; he recalled with remorse the Church's long history of complicity with the powers and dominions that had previously corrupted society. It is a constant matter of self-reflection for churches to have a presence in and dialogue with all parts of society, avoiding the extremes of both sectarian isolation and becoming merely entrenched as a civil religion, a tool of the state (Tomka, 2004, p. 112).

In El Salvador the relationship between Church and society has changed profoundly in recent years. The memory of liberation theology's concern to meet the material and spiritual needs of the oppressed, and of the murder of Archbishop Oscar Romero, has faded. The churches now seem less preoccupied with solidarity with the poorest than with internal divisions and the sharper agendas of evangelical Protestantism (Taylder, 2002, p. 47). Does this not mirror the situation of estranged churches in the West? While society has, as it were, concentrated on its own liberation (or liberalization), the Western Church has become ever more concerned with itself and internal norms, rather than with critiquing its inadequate images of God or developing its role as a radical alternative practice of love.

Jesus acted and spoke with authority, empowering his disciples to reach out to others and to proclaim the Good News (Mark 5.20). The man cured of his demons proceeds to spread (*kerussein*) the good news of all that Jesus has done for him. The Christian Church seems a frail channel indeed for this work of symbolizing how God's relational life is ever more intensely interwoven with the world. Archbishops or the Pope still make the front page when they criticize a world leader, but, except in caricature, the Christian understanding of the mystery of God is largely unknown in the atheistic public life and language that shapes us all.

In the build-up to the second war with Iraq, Alastair Campbell succinctly critiqued the draft of a statement by Tony Blair, 'We don't do God.' It is well known, however, that Prime Minister Blair is a regular worshipper and takes Christian faith seriously. Even though many Christians in business or politics speak wholeheartedly about the future of this planet and its people, the very possibility of doing public theology is strongly contested. The reality that the Church itself often works from inadequate depictions of God and operates from unchristian, authoritarian concepts of authority, raises the question of whether it retains any authority as a symbol and means for human freedom. The task may not even be attractive to many contemporary churches, as it requires the risky choice of acknowledging and receiving the blessings of God for the arduous path of living with ambiguity. The Church sails between the twin dangers of being either so accommodated to its environment as to lose its distinctive voice or so stridently sectarian as to make no authentic connection beyond itself. To follow the path of ambiguity is immediately to perceive the difficulties presented by the wider national and international context; but the rewards could be miraculous, not least in identifying more clearly the failure of confrontational politics, the trust-building effects of dialogue and the envisioning of future possibilities (Childs, 1995, pp. 54ff). Local churches must plan to encourage individual Christians to understand their role in finding possibilities, both for themselves and small groups, to engage with others so as to achieve justice and an ethical approach to international business.

A reflection on Lutheran ecclesiology offers five key notions of the Church's role as a leader and partner in the world in a dialogue on global ethics:

1   Like the international business community itself, the Church and its members transcend national boundaries to constitute an international network with an international mission.

2   The Church is where the people are, at grassroots, in their communities, intimately in touch with the realities of human need so inextricably tied to economic conditions shaped by global business.

3   At its best the Church exists for the benefit of people rather than for its own self-interest. Even the most high-minded corporations, labour unions, industry groups, and the like cannot escape entirely the perspective of their own goals; that is what they exist to promote.

4   The Church is, or should be, free in the security of the gospel promise to model the kind of self-critical openness required for international, multicultural dialogue.

5   The Church has, as the mandate of its love ethic in witness to the coming reign of God, a call to promote reconciliation at all levels of life. Dialogue among parties in a pluralistic world fits that portfolio. (Childs, 1995, p. 143)

Anthony Harvey, in *By What Authority?* (2001), describes the Church's contribution to significant social issues such as urban poverty, marriage, sex and the family. He goes on to argue that Christians can make an authoritative contribution to public policy-making when what they have to say is rooted in the 'admirable' behaviour of Jesus, but with five conditions:

* the task of rectifying human injustices needs to be recognized philosophically as involving the weighing up of complex political realities;
* theological acumen is required to ensure a depth beyond contemporary language and slogans;
* the public debate urgently needs religious insights into the nature of human beings;
* churches need to clarify the kind of exhortations they may legitimately make to the general public who do not claim to share their general faith stance;
* churches have the responsibility to be on the watch for, and to seek redress for, all infringements of human dignity and to work for a world of universal justice.

There is here a question of our moral starting point. If we take an eschatological approach to the nature of and possibilities for humanity, we inevitably collide with the widely held Western utilitarian view in which the greatest good for the greatest number seems to prevail. The Church can only begin to inform public opinion and to reshape the West's perspective once it has embraced its own particular heritage and starting point.

Our approach is based on the belief that the corporate practice of Christian faith should be a vision of authority rooted in obedience to the gospel as the ever-unfolding embodiment of God's being. Despite apparent contrary appearances, it represents God's passionate desire and powerful blessing which informs the reconfiguring of all ways of human life both together and with the planet. Indeed the particular authority of Christian (and indeed Jewish) practice is its accumulation of trustworthy insight and experience concerning the diversity and fullness of human identity. The notion of God and God's presence in the world carries the expectation that in the range of human disciplines and insights there exists a rainbow of wisdom. Moreover, Christian faith and theology can act as a prism, refracting the light of God's presence and the desire to recreate the world in every situation. Churches have a vocation to be, in the particulars of their own life, the practice of authority patterned on Jesus of Nazareth, overshadowed by the Spirit, an advance sign of the social structures in which God would have us flourish.

A vital first stage of re-engaging faith with public life is to listen to stories of how power is exercised and received as authority in business and organizations and to explore where the braided or interwoven learning – that is indeed God's energetic presence – between Church and society might occur.

Who am I?

Increasingly it is recognized that sustainable human work requires attention to both motivation and responsibility for the worker, the client and to the planet. Andrzej Huczynski has researched the beneficial effects of 'influence', upwards, downwards or lateral, compared to the coercive use of authority. His conclusion is that people will do things for others, without being clear about their motivation but with a sense of well-being. People who feel valued will allow themselves to be influenced and led; they may sense they are primarily acting in self-interest, achieving their own personal goals rather than acting for the benefit of the one who influences them (Huczynski and Buchanan, 2001, p. 818).

The collapse of the Western Church's status, wealth and traditional clerical resources are God's current gift. The particular ecclesiological forms that churches deliberately take are crucial signs of the embodied belief about God and about humanity and the world that can inspire all structures for living. Churches over two thousand years have constantly died to particular forms, but as the graced presence of the crucified and risen Christ, are ultimately unstoppable and will re-emerge as they have always done when open to the Spirit. In setting aside an over-concern for 'tomorrow', churches need to challenge and dismantle two persistent dualisms.

The first is the atomistic view of Christian living as an accidental collection of autonomous disciples, or gathering of strangers, seeking individual pastoral consolation and inner meaning, rather than practising church as intrinsically corporate and in immense diversity. This notion of church reflects the long-held perception of the solitary self as an autonomous soul, distinguished in two separate components: physical and mental. Ephesians offers the vision of a dynamic God: the Spirit at work in all for the recapitulation of creation in Christ, when God's sovereignty will be fulfilled. The transformed life of the worshipping community has vast potential to hold authority in society now, through listening to current debates, as well as recalling from within its own memory renewed understandings of social identity.

In an increasingly anonymous and individualized society, in which the slogan is 'you keep out of my life and I'll keep out of yours', to wrestle with the question of identity is an important task. 'Who am I; how am I shaped as a *self*?' How can one be a 'self' when filling so many social roles, moving rapidly from one place to another, engaging with many others who make conflicting demands within a society characterized by complex and consistent change? How is it possible to be authoritatively myself, and at the same time be a person open to webs of relationship that link us ultimately with all of life? The possibility of identifying the 'self' as defined only in relation to other selves is a theme currently being explored in the disciplines of neurophysiology, philosophy, social anthropology and theology. Instead of seeing the self as a private castle, Ricoeur and other philosophers insist that it is a social construction, a locus of multiple difference, and a project rather than a static given.

Those who have theorized about human identity beyond Freud's linking of human motivation largely with biological dynamics, have explored how persons are essentially relating to 'that which is other-than-I'. Authentic personal identity is not primarily a separate, private self, discovered through detachment or through using only those who might be judged to be useful to us, and each of us is constituted as an individual in the matrix of particular times and places. The Object-Relations school insist that relationship is fundamental in human development, while Gestalt psychology offers the challenge that we are not unchanging beings but always in process, inextricably part of the world, discovering ourselves through interaction in all our different facets.

Although he writes primarily on disciplinary power in prisons, the theories of the French philosopher and historian Michel Foucault on institutionalized power seem strikingly relevant in considering how all groups and individuals become 'socially inscribed' and 'normalized' through the everyday expectations of organizations where the 'rules of the game' keep participants in place. Foucault invites everyone to consider their life as a work of art to be deliberately developed, controlled and fashioned. He shows that the self is not the mysterious product of the mind, soul or consciousness, but is known through the embodied acts of the person. So the self, rather than static or alone, is a process with a very uncertain history, both cognitive and emotional.

Christian speech about the person recognizes the self as constantly in formation, becoming, being formed as a creature of God and as one of God's generously self-giving people. However, some aspects of Christian teaching and practice have so emphasized the monotheistic identity and absolute power of God that theological accounts of personhood have naturally overemphasized the autonomous self. A significant corrective notion proposes that we are constituted in our humanness precisely through being recognized as such, in mutuality, by another. The humiliation of prisoners of war in Iraq offers a recent example of the ethical implications of the absence of a relational understanding of personhood. No expression of ethnicity or sexuality is ever just a private matter; no one lives in an incubator and all actions contribute to the common good or evil of political and social networks.

Another corrective identifying the human person in self-possessiveness is articulated by recent extraordinary claims that biblical and Christian theology uniquely provides the resource to bring newness to the world through distinguishing between the concept of the individual and the concept of the person. John Zizioulas, through a detailed reading of the collective Christian experience (as community and in worship, especially the eucharist) and reflection on the communication (*koinonia*) and distinctiveness (*dianerisis*) within the being of God in the early centuries of the Church, speaks with authority of the birth of the 'person' as a relational ontological category. The identity of a particular person is not to be found somewhere deep inside him or her: he has no self, centre, soul, or other form of private existence before being exposed to the world of relationship. The trinitarian persons of God give ultimate demonstration of the way in which we are all constitutive of one another. The personhood of each human is the work of all people in the whole history of the world. To sin is to resist this understanding that divinely created human personhood echoes God's own life as 'communion', by acting as disintegrated and isolated individuals. Human beings enter into their authoritatively true existence through accepting, knowing, mirroring and joining in God's loving, participatory, personal existence (Zizioulas, 1985, pp. 49–51).

A properly conceived doctrine of the Trinity gives a representation of the mystery of God in which the three 'persons' are 'persons' because of their difference from and relation to each other. In God's constant character of love, God freely turns to and gives life to that which is not God. Through God's sustenance, we are persons precisely in our relating to others. Christian faith offers the truth that as persons we exist only in relation to the world, to one another and to God ('members of one another', Ephesians 4.25). This is not a notion of vagueness, or homogeneity, but the belief that in God's provision, in our infinite particularity, we are only truly our unique selves when we are *for* others.

Human nature is not therefore the vague and homogeneous starting point but rather the unique and reciprocal result of who we become in fellowship with God and with all creatures. Authentic human nature develops contingently through taking part, in so far as we implicate ourselves in God's drama of creation, salvation and fulfilment. In risky engagement, interpersonal events and everyday transactions we find our identity and authority. Christian vocation is never a private matter but a response made in freedom to encounters, invitations, blessings and corrections, with deliberate engagement in the process of seeking humankind's true end.

It is a crucial element of the Church's mission in society now to advocate and live out personal being in the light of what God has shown us of our destiny. Contemporary value systems prioritize the individual over against the community, bringing a deep sense of alienation and separation. But the gospel insists that human beings are fundamentally relational and *someone*. The distinctive authority of the Church is to keep alive the practice of biblical 'righteousness'. Christ in his ministry demonstrated how human beings are to be recognized and treated as infinitely loved by God. So gospel communities, formed in the distinctive practice of relationality grounded in the Trinity, oppose the treatment of people simply as grist to the mills of consumerism and efficiency or as dispensable if they have some form of disability.

Faith in the marketplace

In a highly technological and competitive world, Christians struggle to keep an intimate contact with God as the centre of all relating and transforming power. It is one thing to celebrate the central place of God in worship but another to relate this to decisions, ambition, competition, honesty, and all the fears and failings in ourselves and colleagues that arise daily. Having hinted briefly at the polyphony of authority issues that provide the background canvas to this study, we turn our attention to the particular expertise of leadership in industry.

In 1997 Hugh was a director in a subsidiary of a large logistics company when the decision was made to close it. He reflects on the effects on himself, the company and the workers.

The decision to close was a tough one – although economics ultimately dictated it – but the hardest thing was facing our people and giving them the news. It is no easy matter, however well prepared you are and however necessary the action, to look someone in the eye and tell them they are to be put out of work. As a caring Christian I found this even harder, for many complex reasons, although it was the only possible course of action. We were able, almost immediately, to redeploy some staff elsewhere, but the majority of the 350 employees had to be made redundant. Unfortunate as this was, I take a great deal of pride in the positive approach we took. Moreover, as far as possible, all staff were told the news at the same time, concurrently with the clients and with the same message. We had arranged the support of external professionals (paid for by the company) to help individual employees in their search for alternative work and everyone received above the legal minimum pay-off. Remarkably, all those laid off found new jobs immediately or shortly afterwards. I have always been proud of our sensitive approach. Since the company was unprofitable we had to be very focused on closing down the business and yet, despite the apparent ruthlessness of this decision, we were still committed to treating each individual employee with compassion and support.

Michael Edwardes, who was employed to rescue the vehicle manufacturer British Leyland (BL) in 1982, wrote of how, having made the hard decisions without fear or favour, it was then necessary to apply these sympathetically and humanely (Edwardes, 1983). While not faced with problems on the scale of BL, Hugh's experience illustrates the dilemma of balancing care for the employee as an individual person with focused attention to profit and loss, without which there would be no guarantee of survival or the ability to employ anyone (ibid., p. 170).

Committed Christians in industry are increasingly stimulating deep questions about the economy and its impact on people and the world. MODEM – Managerial and Organizational Disciplines for the Enhancement of Ministry – was founded in 1993 to serve both the Church and the business communities generally, by promoting dialogue and sharing insights on good practice. Its focus is on issues such as the impact of new working patterns, the growth of the economy, widening remuneration gaps, the decreasing demand for male manual workers and unskilled people generally, globalization, technology, outsourcing, increases in capital mobility and changes in bargaining power. In the world of the new economy, human worth is measured both in terms of the acquisition of wealth and property and of fulfilment through freedom for leisure and self-development.

Against this backdrop and with the growing and apparently often dehumanizing development of global business, the question arises as to whether business success and integrity are compatible. Christians, and particularly those in business themselves, have a key role in promoting a theology that reflects the reality of work in today's society while reinforcing the need for humanity in dealings with people. The problem lies in satisfying the need for a diverse group of individuals to pull together to achieve organizational objectives while simultaneously recognizing the appropriate work–life balance of each person. We therefore assert the Christian counter-statement that the highest explanation of human 'well-being' arises when all these questions are related to the Spirit-led ordering of God's life in and blessing on the world. Generally, there is a rising tide of ethical concern among contemporary business leaders towards which Christians may make their particular contribution (Childs, 1995).

Religious talk can lack integrity unless it 'seeks to be honest, stays close to the particular, and is rooted in the everyday life of our society' (Sedgwick, 2004, p. 8). Scripture shows how in very human stories, men and women and nations have made meaning of their corporateness through their relationship with God. This interweaving of the story of particular people and communities with the Story of God is no evasion of contingency, complexity and change; fully understood, it offers a radical understanding of deeply committed connectedness. In exploring how organizations and people can act with deep authority in their living, the worship of the trinitarian God is the highest statement of the nature and practice of dynamic relations, the expression of 'love'. Through worship God gives the truth of the meaning of this love to the Church, so offering to all people the possibility of authentic relationality as a contribution to our living together in the world.

Being joined in marriage is more than a bilateral commitment witnessed by the community for the mutual benefit of the couple. The marriage relationship is an expression of God's dynamic, relational movement in them, enabling them to grow with one another and those around them in attention, honesty and intensity. Despite being a mixture of joy and pain, it contributes to the braiding of society as well as bringing fulfilment to those who give themselves to one another. It is the work of the Holy Spirit that energizes God's well-being in the world and creates the world as filled with God's own relational life. Where human life is most vitally authentic, there God is most fully open to affirming and participating in the world and the world is sharing in God's glory.

Corporate authenticity

It is in the nature of all corporate enterprise that complex and competing demands affect the actions of those whose responsibility is to achieve the organization's stated objective. Vision statements for businesses frequently emphasize service or value to the customer. The ultimate objective is to make money, although in the pluralist global culture of the twenty-first century this requires the balancing of a range of demands and approaches. Traditional business leadership was authoritarian. In the late nineteenth century William Lever, for example, was able to view and control the activities of all his key employees from the sanctuary of his office in Port Sunlight. Moreover his authority extended into the village itself, where social norms were highly regulated and displays of excessive individualism could result in dismissal. Lever's paternalistic authoritarianism was far from unique and, although dominating from today's perspective, was benign in comparison to the harsh conditions elsewhere. The balance of power, however, sat very firmly with the employer, and job security was largely unknown even until well after the Second World War.

Complex social and economic changes during the twentieth century increasingly altered the balance between employer and employee, resulting in a more sophisticated understanding and practice of industrial and business management. The needs not only of owners and managers, but of all 'stakeholders', including customers, employees and the wider society, have increasingly been recognized and are reflected both in the rapid growth in research reports and the rise of the management guru.

A key lesson from this consolidated body of learning is that authority can no longer be exercised solely from the centre or top of an organization. The dynamics of performance in organizations depends on the lever pulling or drawing others who are motivated and interested, rather than pushing or driving change. The complex tensions between often competing stakeholder needs require a subtler handling of authority and power. No longer is Marks & Spencer able to rely on customers buying whatever is stocked; local council employers cannot dictate working practices to fire-fighters; the twin Boards of Royal Dutch Shell cannot simply publish estimates of oil reserves without fear of shareholder revolt. These tensions, coupled with the growing size of organizations and greater competition, mean that, throughout business, managers and leaders are having to find new ways of exercising authority, bringing with them the difficulty of maintaining organizational integrity and control while at the same time enabling individuals and sub-units to exercise greater control over their own work and wider future.

This growing tension between centralized authority and decentralization is being aided and driven by technology that facilitates central control while freeing individuals to exercise a degree of creativity over their own working lives and personal needs. Information technology (IT) enables organizations to collect and analyse key data more quickly and accurately than ever before – although, paradoxically, technology also enables new, routine bureaucratic tasks such as time recording, more detailed and current personnel records, collection and processing of statistics, reporting and filing to be introduced, simply because it is now possible to do so.

> In 1988, when Hugh joined a large UK logistics group, corporate accounts took more than a hundred people two weeks every month to produce, and were compiled from a wide range of different manual and computer systems. Today half a dozen people can produce those accounts, far more accurately, in three days.

A key benefit of well-defined processes and use of technology is that leadership can increasingly be focused on ends rather than means. The means increasingly are the defined processes and procedures, the 'hows' of the organization: how to sell, recruit, employ and dismiss; how to keep the accounts; how to maintain a work–life balance; how to maintain equality and fairness; how to manage and avoid stress in the workforce; how to manage purchasing, change, safety, health and environment; and how to engage in the community. Most major retailers have a 'look and feel' that is common across the organization, using standard processes that enable staff to move easily between departments and between outlets. Management's job is to maintain those processes and ensure they are followed, while business leaders, undistracted by the need to fight fires, concentrate on the prophetic, visionary work of mapping the future strategic direction of the business and challenging current practices. The focus of the leader is on recognizing and responding to tensions within the organization and between the organization and its environment, and on shaping responsive strategy. This involves discerning the value of all participants, not merely as impersonal cogs but as individuals with distinct personality and needs. The choreography of the organization is designed by leaders and managers to reach minimum standards in providing value to those who purchase or receive service or information.

Max Scheler describes human beings as 'value-related' in three dimensions in so far as they (1) are vehicles of the supreme value, personal dignity, (2) have a 'natural' need for values which give their existence support, orientation and meaning, and (3) have a capacity for 'perceiving' and 'feeling' values and thus can relate to existing values in a critical and reflective way (Kleinfield, 2000, p. 40). All employees and representatives of organizations carry the meaning of their business in the way they identify with and live out its values. Giving meaning to these corporate values and bringing them to life is an essential function of effective leadership.

A vital ingredient in any corporate life (whether commercial, political or religious) is the capacity for human beings to discover their authority in weighing up, from prevailing values, those by which they will choose to be recognized and bring influence to bear in a particular culture and time. Just as churches are societies that deliberately set out to be embodied public scripts of the gospel, businesses and corporate endeavours disclose in the detail of their operation (the conditions of service for workers, the quality of internal and external communication, care for ecological issues and so on) their corporate sense of culture, the values and principles that guide everyday activity. There is a constant trade-off between political values, economic growth, competitiveness, labour costs, productivity, levels of employment, and conditions of service for workers. Current controversy over the 35-hour week in France and Germany is a case in point (*The Economist*, 31 July 2004, pp. 13ff).

Key questions for all the workers within companies include: 'how can we change the relationship with our customers and suppliers;

what are we here for; is it time for the company to die; how are we going to work differently to accomplish our vision and goal; and how do we organize ourselves for learning?' (Pedler, Burgoyne and Boydell, 1997, p. 55). With marginally different emphasis, these are questions that the Church in many places is already asking of itself, with greater or lesser degrees of success. Business has the resource and authority to deal with these issues in a comprehensive and effective manner that produces not merely academic analysis but effective solutions to real difficulties. The Church has more to learn from this than at times many are willing to acknowledge.

Control comes in many forms. In more traditional power situations the organization that develops has traditionally been hierarchical, led from the top, dominated by heroic personalities and focused less on the needs of individuals within the organization than on the achievement of the organization's goals and the maintenance of its structures. In such organizations power, vested at the centre, is released through the organization in a controlled manner, with the structure being designed to leverage optimum output and control. However, notwithstanding certain notable examples such as Microsoft (Bill Gates), large companies and organizations are increasingly taking the view that no single personality can be 'in charge' and that successful leaders have to be schizophrenic: evaluating and adapting to situations, growing in self-awareness and in awareness of their impact on others, exercising discernment, inventiveness and judgement. The search for heroic figures diverts energy from creating institutions and communities that are able to adapt and reinvent themselves, with leadership arising in many places, not just from the top:

> A new hero-CEO arrives to pump new life into the organization's suffering fortunes. Typically today, the new leader cuts costs (and usually people), and boosts productivity and profit. But the improvements do not last. Many of the leader's grand strategies never get implemented; instead people cling to habitual ways of doing things. Sooner or later, new crises ensue, giving rise to the search for new hero-leaders. In effect, the myth of the hero-leader creates a reinforcing vicious spiral of dramatic changes imposed from the top, and diminished leadership capacity in the organization, leading eventually to new crises and yet more heroic leaders. (Senge, 1999, pp. 11–12)

In a fluid and shifting context, hierarchies of importance are being replaced by reliance on expert power; instead of those in charge, it is those with the deepest understanding of the problems who are taking the decisions (Huczynski and Buchanan, 2001, p. 804). Against a background of compressed timescales, the growing importance of information and, more critically, of processed, analysed, synthesized and modelled knowledge and intelligence should not be underestimated. In the resulting hostile climate, survival depends on decentralized decision-making.

A major UK retailer a few years ago needed to find a new supplier to store and distribute one of its ranges of household products at short notice. A particular company was approached and a contract agreed in late January. As no suitable warehouse was immediately available internally, a search was undertaken and a partially derelict site identified and taken over for renovation on 9 February. The first product began to be distributed from the site on 26 February. All services, including telephones and IT communication, had to be installed within those 17 days. In order to achieve this, a huge degree of autonomy had to be given to the managers and staff on site. Central control of any aspect of this development could have significantly delayed implementation.

Leadership is a key issue for all modern organizations. Old style 'command and control' is largely redundant, although the implementation of technology has introduced more subtle forms of this approach to leadership. Notwithstanding this, discussion continues on the future of leadership and increasingly this looks beyond the simple needs of the organization and recognizes the complex web of interrelationships in which all organizations are engaged.

A vital area to which attention is increasingly paid in consultations on future leadership carried out by organizations of many kinds, relates to ethical challenges. This is as keenly true for business as for other types of organization often more closely associated with the ethics of public consciousness, such as medicine and justice. At the heart of any commercial undertaking is the vital ambition to create wealth but the acquisition of wealth in its own right has been regarded by Christians and others as at best somehow shoddy or rather unpleasant, and at worst unethical and self-seeking. Making a gain from trading has been a fundamental strand of many cultures, yet only a minority of religious teachers have addressed the consequent ethical issues.

In an increasingly complex world of credit, banking and universal trade, lost innocence cannot be regained. However, a dilemma faces Christians when conditions of human thriving are brushed aside for the single goal of wealth creation for the few. The continuing Thatcherite legacy of living for one's own benefit alone, and events such as the Enron scandal and the embezzlement scandals of the early 1990s, have done little to improve the image of large enterprise in a world where capital knows no boundaries, and pays little respect to national governments or the needs of particular countries or peoples. Large companies have great power, are quickly able to move work and capital from one side of the world to the other and to lay off large numbers of people. In the 1980s coal jobs were effectively exported to Poland and other Eastern European countries, while more recent examples are the move of 'knowledge' jobs from banks, IT services and retail call centres in the UK to India and South Korea. Such momentous changes can have an adverse effect on the way people perceive industry, reinforcing perceptions caused by failing pension funds or poor health and safety.

This is not to argue that public opinion is entirely anti-business. Reality is more complex. The entire population is involved directly with business either as consumer or employee, or both, giving some degree of sophistication in perceptions of the value of business and industry. However business and enterprise, capital and labour are viewed, there are some wider key issues for society to which the churches can make a significant contribution. For many, the experience of work is burdensome and driven largely by self-interest. The purpose of business is to make money and yet the process of doing so introduces responsibilities and more complex needs and agendas, not merely for shareholders (the owners) but for employees and society at large. For example, is finance the only consideration for a company marketing dangerous pesticides in poor countries unable to afford the enforcement of those safety standards that obtain in affluent countries? (Childs, 1995, p. 36).

From a theological point of view, how is it possible to hold together a focus on profit (without which no one will continue to be employed or to fulfil their human economic responsibilities) and the possibility of living authentically in the love of God that fills the world, transforming people, cultures and places? The prophetic religions – Judaism, Christianity and Islam – carry the potential and responsibility for understanding and nurturing true human selfhood and action.

Why?

A commonly asked question is 'Couldn't we do this better?' A more perceptive question would be 'Can't we find a better way of doing this?' Central, however, to any consideration of authority is the question 'Why?' which relates to the most deeply held values of the organization. Why are we spending all this time, money and resource in doing this? Is this the best thing we might be doing at all?

Another common thread to emerge is the growing recognition that in existing, maturing and working we are bound to one another in fields, systems, teams and relationships. No single analogy for God can ever stand too much weight. The recent reclaiming of the Christian concept of the Trinity, however, offers a wide range of language and images evoking a sense of God's life as the dynamic transforming energy among all creatures. The metaphor of a dance is increasingly used to describe the trinitarian livingness of God, and the intimacy of humanity and creation with God and with one another. Another image that might be used is that of friendship. Difference in relationship as 'friendship', as a mirror of the love that God is and gives to the world, has the capacity for releasing us from domination and absence of genuine contact.

For the Christian Church dispersed in society, the purpose and the way of working, the outcome and the process are one: to disclose God's love in the world. It is hardly surprising that the authority of Christian community living is such a high priority as a way of modelling and yearning for hope in a world deeply fragmented by shallow public and global relationships. Community means the death of the observer and the commitment of becoming a participant. As Dietrich Bonhoeffer reminded us, when we criticize the body of the Church it is our own selves (dying and risen in Christ) we are blaming. The community of disciples has the responsibility, at whatever cost, to be a God-shaped agency for bringing to our world refuges for those in danger, channels for recognizing and developing gifts and a mosaic of different people that point to the triune life of Godself. Eucharist, worship, song, scripture, deep prayer, self-reflection, shared meals, forgiveness, coming and going, at their best bring wholeness and peace to the Church. Down the centuries Christian pioneers have demonstrated how the practice of such community life puts down living wells of hope for the world's potential. We see this in every authentic and stretching instance of local church, notably in the work of Martin Luther King's appeal for freedom for all. Despite fear of government reprisal, rain and tiredness, marchers sang, swayed and clapped irrepressibly, 'a group of paupers but prouder than kings' (Dear, 1998, p. 79).

The list of pioneering leaders for community pregnant with God's life is endless but for us must include El Salvador's martyred Archbishop Oscar Romero, working with all his energy alongside Christ for the salvation of the world in every concrete detail; the Friars Minor of St Francis of Assisi; Gustavo Gutiérrez's liberation theology of warm, affectionate, caring relationships; and Jean Vanier's L'Arche, intimate communities of acceptance of those the world pushes to one side. Christians in business can make a living without treating others as 'the enemy who has to be undermined or discredited' (Childs, 1995, p. 1).

At the heart of authoritative, God-shaped living is the peace with the Other that replaces adversarial rivalry and the amazing recognition that others are not in reality hateful, stupid, or a threat because they are different. They will certainly shatter the certainties of life as we have known it up to this moment, but the result of this disclosure for our growing and deepening will always be beyond our wildest imagination. The Egyptian poet C. P. Cavafy (1863–1933) encapsulates this fear and possibility in 'Waiting for the Barbarians'. In the forum the Emperor and titled citizens wait from early dawn in spectacular and frightening array, but are speechless and resigned to being overrun 'because the barbarians are coming today'. At dusk, with the non-arrival of the barbarians, their mood turns to bewilderment and confusion as in a way the barbarians had seemed the ideal solution to their own problems (Astley, 2003, pp. 339–40).

2 | Energy

Social change

Loneliness and isolation are the bitter experience of many in contemporary Western society. Government social policies increasingly focus on protecting citizens from one another through CCTV, or on the defence of ourselves against intruders to our homes or from those on sex offender lists who live round the corner. Binge drinking and other addictions are ways of escaping the pain and despair that, in a disordered culture, life makes no sense. Churches are often prominent partners among those offering relief and encouragement to those on the edge. However, our developing theology of power suggests that beyond the offer of relief, the Church has a duty to critique and contribute to the urgent search for alternative ways of living together in hope. An attempt at a concise definition of society might be 'a set of meanings structured in particular social patterns', although Margaret Thatcher's famous claim still lingers, that the notion of 'society' is a liberal fiction. In the West there is still energy in the debate about whether the state is the villain, a burden on families, or whether the community can exist not only in small face-to-face groups but also within the entire matrix of a nation or the world. Rather than an uncritical devotion to the notion of a benign state or political party, the way forward lies beyond old political and economic alignments.

Contemporary debate on a renewed appreciation of 'dwelling' or 'place' takes us beyond naïve nostalgia for the days of innocence. Power in relation is a vital key to working effectively on the values and practices that make for humaneness in any situation. Consideration of physical locations, institutions, or nations and the relation between races, raises the question of the quality of relatedness required for truly inhabiting any situation, rather than merely co-existing, either in adversarial or laissez-faire ambience. 'Community' is frequently caricatured as symbolizing no more than soft idealism and as the opposite of serious hard-headed realism. Building on what we have learned so far, suppose it were identified instead in terms of the ways in which many differing people offer life in abundance through all the ways they choose to occupy locations together. The biblical and holistic concept of excess, blessing or 'life in abundance' suggests a search for particular forms of social life, rather than the mere espousal of one human grouping or party over another:

> To *inhabit* a place is to dwell there in a practised way, in a way which relies upon certain regular, trusted habits of behaviour. Our prevailing, individualistic frame of mind has led us to forget this root sense of the concept of 'inhabitation'. We take it for granted that the way we live in a place is a matter of individual choice (more or less regulated by bureaucratic regulations). (Inge, 2003, p. 131)

What does the Church bring to this quest for community from its particular experience? For the Christian, baptism and eucharist are sacramental ways of allowing God to inscribe in human living the benefits of daring face-to-face encounter as the key to life in every sphere – not just in small intimate groups. Together, in repentance and expectation, Christians grow in faith, as water is condensed, becoming a purposeful place shaped by God, a *habitus* occupied by Christ. So God's people accept the joyful responsibility of offering this gospel-shaped pattern as a major contribution to the renewal of the universe.

There can be no simple, objective definition of a society, created as it is through conflicting and many-layered meanings. National boundaries are becoming increasingly less important in any meaningful definition of a group of people. Governments may retain considerable power (as authority), but while their ability to circumscribe individual action and behaviour has increased through the application of technology (databases of population, surveillance, identity cards), their own actions are also increasingly circumscribed by wider authority. Membership of the European Union (EU) and acceptance of international norms of legal behaviour either by treaty (for example on human rights) or by tacit acceptance (such as UN Mandate) supersede or at least modify the behaviour of governments.

While such explicit ceding of authority is important, what might be described as 'implicit loss of authority' is also increasingly influential, not only on the part of government but on the whole of society and the idea of the nation state. At the extreme, terrorist associations and groupings (such as al-Qaeda) are examples of implicit authorities. Although such organizations appear increasingly to drive the actions of governments and supra-governments (EU, UN), they are fortunately not the main authorities informing and acting across national boundaries. Enabled particularly by technology, business and commercial organizations are, in practice, a much greater and more significant source of international authority. The movement of capital, for example, is a key driver of change in society (Lynch, 2003, pp. 528ff). The movement of jobs between countries, the setting up of call centres on the far side of the world or the international nature of manufacturing (a car sold in the UK is the product of work carried out in many countries) reflect the changing nature of international business and commerce and their effect on the traditional nation state.

While not the sole causes of change, cheap fuel and international relations are key enablers of social, cultural, moral and philosophical movements in the West. The availability of cheap goods and services enables people to see the possibility and often the partial realization of a better standard of living. A key element in understanding the place of energy as power is that, while cheap energy and changing relationships are enablers, there is a sense in which they also become the engines of change. The ease with which needs can be gratified allows a growth in ambition for gratification of further need (real or perceived).

The growth of multi-national companies is no coincidence, for the satisfaction of large-scale demand requires appropriately complex operations and conversely such operational scale traditionally brings economies that drive down cost. Since 1980, for example, there has been a huge shift in the way that manufacturing companies operate with production of particular items increasingly centralized in one country (Ohmae, 1990). The rebranding, for example, of Mars' 'Marathon' as 'Snickers' is a reflection of the manufacturer's need to obtain production economies of scale by producing a single confectionery product in one factory but saleable in many markets. But the growth of the large multi-national manufacturer is not merely a response to a business opportunity; it also reflects a major shift in the balance of power between manufacturer, retailer and consumer. In Hungary, for example, Tesco sells almost exclusively own-label products, in marked contrast to the UK where consumer demand for branded goods (as opposed to supermarket own label) remains very high. Manufacturers such as Heinz, Unilever and Kellogg's continue to spend enormous sums on brand advertising, thus maintaining consumer demand for their products.

In order to enable the uninterrupted delivery of those goods and services which will meet consumer demand, the availability of effective, timely and accurate information and knowledge is critical. The centralization of manufacturing, sourcing from the far side of the world, constantly changing fashion, and fickle consumer buying all demand the ability of systems to respond rapidly to change. Modern networked IT systems not only facilitate but also positively enable this (see also Chapter 3). Such changes in manufacturing are reflected in many service sectors and the impact on both jobs and wider society is considerable (Golzen, 1983, ch. 2).

The complexities of social change are found in a whirl of ideas, knowledge, information, observation and past experience. At the macro level the ability to change requires mechanisms to meet demand. Part of the current Western situation is that demand far outstrips what is essential for maintenance of life, so causing unjust imbalances in the availability of basic necessities worldwide. The changing balance between national government and wider transnational authority is a key element in social change, but ultimately society is formed through the complex ways in which people and organizations choose to interrelate. Just as organizations depend on fallible human beings in all their multitudinous character, so society is a cauldron of individual demand, ego and constantly emerging identity.

As we have explored, Western preoccupation with *self* is a constant challenge to a Christian theological perspective on the meanings that inhabit the behaviours of individuals and organizations. In comparison with, say, African societies, Westerners strive in the competitive pursuit of individual and family health, wealth and happiness. Writing about the challenge of Japanese competition, Ezra Vogel measured well the self-confident American desire to be overall 'winners' when he invented the title *Japan as Number One* (Morgan, 1997, p. 126). The world's preoccupation with the economic growth of some countries at the expense of others is mirrored in some individualistic and narcissistic spiritual patterns. Working practices however show an increase in co-operation for mutual benefit, such as to create a measure of shared decision-making and control, pool expertise or share risk in research and development, through numerous kinds of informal networking (ibid., p. 65).

However, the rapid pace of life, the dispersed nature of relationships and the complexity of interrelationships, moderated by people over whom we have little or no control and no access (decision makers in banks, government, the stock market, our supermarket, social services) means that much of our emotional energy is expended on our own dilemmas.

Task focused organization

Commercial businesses of all kinds exist to make money (a profit) and this is the primary reason for their existence, although Peter Drucker argues that what is critical is not so much the making of a profit as the avoidance of loss (Drucker, 1955, p. 64). In practice, of course, company activities are, among other constraints, circumscribed by regulation, competition and ethical considerations. The work of charities, sporting and environmental causes would be severely limited without the sponsorship of businesses. However, given that profit is their primary focus and that unprofitable companies don't survive, are there implications for a Church with the primary focus of working for God's purposes in the world? Within the Church there is a frequently expressed denial that commercial enterprises can provide any insights for the Church, just as there are Christians whose ecclesiology rebuts serious engagement between faith and the workplace (Clitherow, 2004, pp. 36–8).

Clitherow's passion for a rediscovery of God's holiness doesn't necessarily create a false polarity between piety and the outworn fantasies of Fordist-shaped managerialism. God's ways in the world leave no room for a disjuncture between God and a disembodied holiness. An interweaving of theological and organizational theory makes it possible for churches to be as properly concerned with developing the clarity of purpose associated with effectiveness as with patterns of relating that honour everyone concerned. Despite the usually very different objectives of business and church, dialogue has the potential for mutual benefit. In consequence, the Church receives access to practical and relevant models, attitudes and approaches, while organizations may access renewed energy from a reappraisal of working practices critiqued by Christian faith. The holiness and truth of God are, in reality, at the heart of every worthwhile endeavour, and can be known in the entire spectrum of humanist disciplines.

A common perception to be challenged suggests that business organizations are homogeneous structures, peopled by automatons, a 'corporate animal', the product of a single mould. Recognizing and appreciating the range of difference, and the differing motivations of individuals, within organizations of all kinds (but particularly in business) has been the object of considerable research.

Productivity gains were significant when the pioneering American Quaker engineer, Frederick W. Taylor (1856–1915), deconstructed jobs into simple repetitive tasks designed to increase productivity. However, in the longer term the dehumanizing effects of 'Scientific Management' resulted in a falling away of productivity. The key flaw in Taylor's approach was the failure to recognize the immense difference between people and to realize that, while the energy level of the organization as a whole might increase (as measured by its output), the detrimental effect on individuals could be significant. From a corporate perspective, in an environment in which labour was plentiful and cheap the wastage of individuals was considered an acceptable cost. Although now generally regarded as intolerable, the legacy, and accompanying fear, of Scientific Management still remains.

George Myerson, exploring the impact of mobile-phone technology on human intercommunication, in dialogue with Jürgen Habermas highlights two contrasting twentieth-century concepts of common enterprise: system integration and social integration. He contrasts 'system integration', where people are glued together by common procedures and rules, with 'social integration', where people stay together through a common understanding that they keep working out among themselves.

Myerson (2003) has developed the view that electronic systems and procedures subvert 'normal' human social interaction and communication. However, his theory needs to be tempered by the sight in any public place of relaxed young people, relating innovatively through the process of exchanging text messages and digital photographs. The debate is heightened if, while a group of people are sitting together at table, one member is mostly engaged in a conversation by text and disengaged from the group. Overemphasis on process and reliance on IT clearly has the potential to dehumanize relationships by reducing the intensity of immediate presence between people (Deal and Kennedy, 2000, p. 146).

The most immediate example of a procedurally driven organization is one that deals with money, such as a bank, building society, business or government department. Financial management has long been among the most tightly process-driven functions of business organizations. Increasingly, however, other key processes are being similarly systematized, often globally, through the introduction of technology in ways never previously envisaged. The result is that all the key processes in an organization can be interlocked to give a degree of control never previously seen. Processes associated with manufacturing, marketing, management, finance, people management, sales, raw materials, warehousing, transport and any other function an organization may require can be so integrated using IT that information collected in one area is immediately available for all others. This not only removes the need repeatedly to record the same data but also changes fundamentally the nature of work and, more particularly, the ability of the organization to respond rapidly to change.

Complex forces drive the need for formalized procedures, not least legislation that demands ever tighter and fairer treatment of individuals. Sexual and racial discrimination, employment protection, health and safety, child protection, work-time directives and data protection as well as financial constraints, coupled with an increasingly litigious population, all require organizations of all kinds to be increasingly protective. This further drives the need for, and the use of, formal information systems. Even within small organizations, not able to afford complex IT resources, manual processes are no longer adequate for the degree of accurate record keeping and data processing now required. At one level such systems release employees to engage in less mundane and bureaucratic activity. While this increases both productivity and the sense of organizational achievement, paradoxically standardization also removes some of the quirkiness, the individualism of human behaviour, the difference that makes work interesting and satisfying for the individual. This can be either energy-sapping or energy-enhancing, depending on the degree to which the individual has control over their own actions and on the type of person they are.

We shall consider this in more detail later in this chapter when we discuss Meredith Belbin's work on teams.

While Taylor's notion of scientific management had a dehumanizing effect on work by forcing people to concentrate on small and very particular elements of a task, modern approaches to systems, though removing the most tedious components, have to a degree retained practices of control and segmentation. Although technology to an extent liberates people from tedious tasks, replacing it by the possibility of more productive and wide-ranging work, in a different and perhaps less clear way it may continue to de-energize people by its structured and circumscribing approach.

In contrast to Taylor's concentration on the needs of the task (largely at the expense of employees hired to achieve it), A. H. Maslow and Frederick Herzberg have studied human needs and in particular those that increase motivation (Maslow, 1971; Herzberg, 1968). Maslow's central argument lies in what he described as a hierarchy of needs: (1) physiological, (2) safety, (3) belongingness, (4) aesthetics, (5) learning and discovery, (6) esteem, (7) self-actualization, and finally (8) transcendence.

His research suggests that, before social interaction can be on the agenda, people must first satisfy the most primitive requirements of safety and security. For a person to become highly motivated, first the lower needs and then the need for esteem and self-actualization (that is self-fulfilment) must also be met. Those who are fully energized are those who have worked their way through the hierarchy of needs. This thesis, while sometimes criticized as oversimplistic and often challenged by those who selflessly give of themselves, still resonates with a Church that values the individual as one formed in relationship with and in the image of the living God.

The Trappist M. Basil Pennington offers a parallel distilled from the wisdom of Thomas Aquinas and, behind him, the Byzantine Christian theologian St John of Damascus. His suggestion is that leading up to a period approximately three thousand years ago, human life graduated through several stages of development and aspiration and, in a parallel way, this pattern may also be one for each person to travel through in a lifetime. He identifies a range of categories from 'pure matter to Divine Spirit':

Alpha Period: dawning of human consciousness
Beta Period: bodily consciousness
Gamma Period: group consciousness
Iota Period: individual consciousness
Tau Period: transcendent consciousness
Omega Period: unitive consciousness.

His urgent summons to the contemporary world is that this is a time for choosing:

> We live within the Iota Period. It is a decisive time. We can move ahead to integration, transcendence, and consummation. Or we can fall back and seek our fulfilment in the quests of earlier periods: survival, pleasure, and power. We see the struggle all about us. It is a time of choice. And each one of us can make a difference. Each one of us seeking transcendence through personal integration and meditation raises the whole. This is what Jesus was on about when he spoke of us as leaven. (Pennington, 2000, pp. 60–1)

Building on Maslow's work, Frederick Herzberg germinated the idea of 'hygiene factors', that is, those things that actively demotivate by their absence rather than motivate by their presence. So, for example, the absence of money or an unfair or inadequate wage will demotivate an individual but conversely, significantly increasing financial reward may have no positive effect on motivation. Primo Levi, a Jewish survivor of Auschwitz, illustrates the basic truth of Maslow's thesis. When all has been removed, even the prospect of life, a person's focus is not on accumulation of wealth, or even the support of other human beings, but on the most basic personal survival. Levi describes in the gentlest ways the absolute concentration on getting through the day and, beyond that, the winter cold. It is only once spring arrives and with it some prospect of warmth that the prisoners can concentrate on anything else (Levi, [1958, 1963] 1979).

We have explored how energy within organizations can increase through focusing on the task (Taylor) or on the people involved (Maslow and Herzberg). Frequently overlooked are the organizational and personal relationships within the team. Families, tribes and military units evoke increasing loyalty in times of crisis. René

Girard however has shown that institutions in crisis tend to deny the functional difference and diversity between people (Storrs, 2004, pp. 9ff). It is of immense significance, therefore, that Meredith Belbin has pioneered the exploration of team dynamics. His theories distinguish teams from groups, principally by size but also recognizing the commonality of purpose, specific individual roles and methods of selection that tend to characterize the team. His theories of team roles challenge leaders to recognize how different people react more positively in different scenarios and to allow them sufficient space to play to their strengths, rather than forcing them into unfamiliar and uncomfortable ways of working (Belbin, 1996a, b).

Belbin argues that individuals have preferred ways of working or 'patterns of contribution' within teams and he identifies a number of types of contribution or team roles. Most people are able to handle a number of these roles under varying conditions and are, to some degree, able to adopt different roles according to the mix of preferences available in any given team. Unlike most psychometric tests (such as Myers–Briggs or 16PF) which concentrate on individual preferences, Belbin's work is based on the combined and complementary preferences of any given team, such that those with a balanced mix of preferences across all characteristics are more likely to work effectively as a team.

Belbin's original work identified eight characteristics; a further technical role, that of 'Specialist', was subsequently added. Inevitably any label used to describe people or their roles risks misinterpretation as all words are loaded with meaning for the particular reader. Belbin has taken some care to amend his titles over the years, finely tuning them in a particular technical sense. The roles, described below, are not 'jobs' in the team but contributions that all or some within the team may make:

- Coordinator: coordinates the team's efforts, motivates and clarifies goals and priorities
- Shaper: imparts drive, challenges, pressurizes, finds ways round obstacles
- Plant: creates original ideas, solves difficult problems
- Resource investigator: explores resources and new possibilities, develops contacts, negotiates
- Monitor/evaluator: evaluates options, analyses, judges likely outcomes

- Implementer: organizes the work, turns ideas into practical forms
- Completer/finisher: follows up on detail, searches out errors, omissions, oversights, concentrates on and keeps others to schedules and targets
- Teamworker: supports others, listens, builds, averts friction, handles difficult people
- Specialist: provides expertise, knowledge and technical skills that are in rare supply

Another approach works from the necessity of facing reality by tapping into 'our dreams and ideal visions of our lives'. Groups begin to change only when they first have fully grasped the reality of how they function, particularly when individuals in the group recognize that they are working in situations that are dissonant or uncomfortable. It is critical that they understand this reality on an emotional, even visceral, level (Goleman, Boyatzis and McKee, 2002, p. 172). Goleman believes groups only begin to function correctly and to develop a proper vision for themselves when each participant is attuned to the others' personal visions, so creating an 'emotionally intelligent, resonant, and more effective group' (ibid., p. 173). Essential group norms, or core values, are the often implicit rules by which groups and teams organize themselves and are especially relevant during the management of change. Teams that not only understand their own core values but are able to recognize and respond to external and internal stimuli, are likely to respond more quickly and effectively than conventional teams (ibid., 2002, ch. 9). In Chapter 5 we shall develop this notion of flexible teams in terms of 'Adaptivity'.

Redundant energy

Organizations of different sizes are faced with challenges that drain emotional energy. For commercial enterprises this reveals itself in the constant drive to 'do more with less', to 'work smarter' (*sic*), to become more efficient, and to increase productivity. At a primitive level this is represented by (revolutionary or evolutionary) organizational change resulting frequently in workforce reduction. Organizations facing critical change are often driven both by financial concerns and in response to changing circumstances, possibly a fundamental change in the business model (market change, merger, takeover, competition, restructuring, new management seeking to make a mark). It is rare for a workforce to be entirely ignorant of at least the context of change. Managers and employees fully appreciate the profit and cost drivers and key performance indicators that show a worsening situation. Major change is often openly presaged by tighter cost control, reductions in training, more process and a less easy working environment, as well as a culture that gives advance warning that something is likely to happen. The more effective teams manage these situations with care for the people, ensuring that messages are delivered in a timely and uniform manner.

Despite the surge of growth in jobs within the UK economy during the late 1990s and early 2000s, redundancy persists and is the most obvious outcome of organizational change. Major structural changes associated with redundancy and outsourcing are inevitably prime causes for the loss of emotional energy within an organization and the more rapid and dramatic the change, the greater the negative impact and the time it takes the organization to recover. For differing personalities among those selected for redundancy, a combination of emotions including fear, anger, denial and loss of self-esteem may arise, as well as resignation or even relief that the waiting is over. But the emotions of redundancy are not limited to those who leave. Experience shows that the impact may be greater on those left behind. Hugh is aware of a preference among managers for euphemisms such as 'slim down', 'focus on core activity', or 'outsource', which reflects deeper tensions, leading him to consider the degree of discomfort felt by those who expect to survive redundancy processes. For those who have to make redundancy decisions and inform the individuals involved, the stress can impact on both professional and personal lives. Ensuring that people have mutual support from others in the same situation, as well as professional advisers, is critical for the overall focus and effectiveness of the organization during a time of uncertainty and potential chaos.

Irrespective of the care taken in its planning, major structural change, particularly removing a large part of the workforce, either through redundancy or outsourcing, is hugely disruptive. The situation means that critical work is often not done, processes that previously worked seamlessly break down, social networks unravel and leadership is found to be missing in key places. An organization can lose a great deal of energy as people and processes slowly realign to meet a new challenge and changed expectations.

'Outsourcing', referred to above, is an increasingly familiar trend. This is the process by which businesses and institutions contract out specific services, previously run internally, to specialist suppliers. Outsourcing can occur in any non-core area of a business such as catering, cleaning, security, IT, sub-assembly manufacture or call centres. Under UK law, staff normally have the right to transfer to the new entity under the same terms and conditions which they previously enjoyed. In the medium term the impact on the behaviour and emotional energy of outsourced individuals can be negative, as the new employer seeks to drive down costs and increase productivity in an environment that may be alien to the transferred workforce. So, for example, civil servants transferred to the private sector under the government's Transfer of Undertakings (Protection of Employment) Regulations 1981 – generally known as TUPE – while retaining their former terms and conditions of employment, may face a quite different cultural approach and motivation to work within the new organization. This may lead to problems both for the organization that has to deal with these issues and for the individuals involved.

For the leadership of any organization undergoing significant change it is crucial for those 'left behind' that the redundancy process is ethical (that the basis of selection is fair and understood), structured and properly supported. Although 50 or even 25 years ago redundancy was often considered a bar to future employment, today it has become relatively 'normal', yet the impact on everyone involved remains high.

The effects of structural change, particularly when redundancy or other forms of 'downsizing' are involved, can be so debilitating that any wise organization wishing to encourage successful change in a short period will engage with its employees (those leaving as well as those who remain) with professional sensitivity. The trauma of repeated change threatens the focus of the organization and fosters defensive behaviours that debilitate the very changes being undertaken. Language is a key element in the task of constantly re-energizing an organization.

Some years ago Hugh invited a senior director of his employer to address his team of some 40 people. The team had worked extremely hard to turn round a difficult situation and the aim of the address was to re-energize the members through affirmation of their work and recognition of their contribution. The first three-quarters of the meeting met this aim. However, the director suddenly added, 'Of course, things are very difficult at the moment and there will be more redundancies.' The effect was stunning and immediate, completely undermining the positive work done earlier. The use of language is a highly skilled element within the role and skills of leaders. In order not to deceive or frighten the workforce, carefully worded statements are required to increase positive energy. Realities have to be faced and communicated. Bad news delivered in person, at a well-chosen time and with full recognition of the likely impact on individual people as well as on the organization, can ameliorate a potentially damaging situation.

The churn in jobs caused by major economic changes in work has a number of effects on society, both positive and negative. While the growth in the number of part-time and lower-paid jobs might be seen as negative, the UK economy in the early part of the twenty-first century reports the lowest unemployment figures for more than 20 years (Government figures, April 2004). While employment may bring income and purpose to some who might otherwise be fully dependent on state benefits, there is concern that low-paid jobs frequently demand little skill and, for many, are unfulfilling. The discussion of Maslow's hierarchy of need showed that people's motivation generally increases as they move towards 'self-actualization', that is when they are, holistically speaking, delivering at their full potential. In Christian theological terms, we assert that God creates people for a purpose and fulfilment lies in knowing, accepting and responding. An effective base for a long-term, stable and productive (in the widest sense of that word) society does not include escalating numbers of low-paid, unfulfilling jobs of uncertain security. Emotional energy is generated, not in the fulfilment of productive mutual activity, but rather in the satisfaction of personal need, often of the most basic kind.

A further trend that can have an adverse effect on emotional energy is the move towards 'industrialization' based on standardization of processes and procedures. As we saw in relation to the theories of Taylor, cost effectiveness for management is not even a medium-term success strategy. Simply to manoeuvre people to ensure that failures in process are quickly identified and corrected is a form of control and use of people as a means to an end which is intolerable within a Christian understanding of God's ways with the world. Managers argue that working in such an organization can be fulfilling and safe (so far as any job today is safe) in that the parameters, rules, frameworks, processes and procedures are all clearly defined. This means not only that individuals can find their way round more easily but that teams containing the wide range of differing skills identified by Belbin can be assembled quickly to meet new challenges and become productive very rapidly without the overhead of trying to agree ways of working. However, in terms of emotional energy, or Christian theology, the ignoring of personal needs severely limits the satisfaction that even secular theorists have insisted is essential for a successful enterprise.

Humane working

We are taking it as axiomatic that the Church has the responsibility and potential to inspire and demonstrate, from its faith and practice, how humans might better live and work together within the world's ecology. The ways the Church handles its own present struggles is a sharp test of its capacity to fulfil that wider vocation. Church leaders, surveys and reports advocate strategies for growth in a 'mission-shaped church' and 'new expressions' of church. This is in the context of widespread anxiety about 'managing decline' or a resignation to the present difficulties. Numbers of worshippers are falling, finances worrying, and there are insufficient clergy to staff the current model of church. The stark facts are overlaid by competing narratives about their significance. Historians cannot demonstrate a period in history when the Church has not had its institutional worries and conflicts. We believe that the current Church increases its panic when it chooses either to listen only to humanistic disciplines or to ignore them. Some believe that human organizational insight does not connect with God's truth and holiness. There is a seductive tendency to polarize management and holiness, as though pastoral care or mission planning are above mundane matters like quality control or value for money (Clitherow, 2004, p. 10). We recognize this risk but believe God's life can be mediated best through an interdisciplinary rather than a dualistic framework. All organizations, including the Church, are called to understand their development in the light of the meaning to be found in the gospel of Jesus Christ and therefore of God. The long association between incompetent otherworldliness and Christian faith, often lampooned in the media and drama, should evoke an urgency to reappraise the connection between 'religious' and 'worldly' organizational concepts and activity. Church and human organizational practice until recently have often overlapped. It is a false dichotomy that places individual pious practice in a vacuum; while a theology too related to static and hierarchical notions of power denies the creative potential of overlap and recip-rocation in nurturing social practices that develop capable, mutually relating and well-motivated people (Lynch, 2003). Open-ended research by MODEM (2002) produced evidence pointing to the conditions which best facilitated the release of spiritual energy among managers and groups within an organization. Some of the initial assumptions were that

1   Persons are best understood as whole beings with intercon-nected physical, mental, emotional and spiritual aspects.
2   It is the spiritual aspect of persons, and the spiritual energy at work within them, that is the least well understood and most in need of investigation.
3   Something, which may be called the spirit of an organization, is derived from the deep bonds occurring when people share common values, principles and a sense of purpose greater than themselves.
4   The spiritual energy in persons and the spirit of an organization may serve purposes which are good or evil, and the ethical eval-uation of the purposes at work is therefore very significant in investigating the spiritual aspect of persons and organizations.

The research conclusions found that corporate energy arises from confidence in a common purpose, that the flow of energy is pro-moted when the vision, the culture, the values, the ground rules are all crucial aspects of the context, liberating and enabling people to pull together to make things better in the future. Energy soars when there is collective belief and confidence, people are treated as equals, and trust, empowerment, self-motivation and fulfilment are ingredients. In addition, the research spoke of power as interactive energy, fusion, chain reaction, and as both elusive and mysterious. Furthermore, this investigation highlighted three primary conditions for the release of exceptional energy: an inspiring purpose, a liberating and empowering context, and an attitude of hope, confidence and commitment. Finally it has been suggested that spirituality, rather than something to be pursued internally or in isolation, is truly about interconnectedness with self, others, nature or the environment, and God. The MODEM investigation indicated clearly how participants were being connected to self (e.g. self-confidence and commitment), to others (e.g. synergy in the group), but evidence did not point to relationality with nature or the environment and participants were reticent in identifying the source of the energy (Pettifer, 2002).

In a society that often chooses not to integrate the meaning that Christians find in God with ordinary political, economic and business dealings, a possible connecting route may lie in the widespread interest in human self-development. Many therapy and counselling organizations, espousing no particular religious language, and even denying the validity of a transcendent perspective, have a profound concern for helping people to find their inner energy. The pursuit of human flourishing, the healing of memories, the rediscovery of parts of a person that have become hidden or dormant, are the focus of a variety of therapeutic disciplines, for individuals and groups.

We believe the Christian Church has sufficient resources and integrity to work with these disciplines without denying its own unique contribution (Greenwood, 2002, pp. 54ff). Indeed an outstanding example of such practice is St Beuno's Retreat Centre in North Wales where every aspect of human flourishing, and proven human disciplines and insights, are integrated with an Ignatian (affective) approach to inner awakening. So, in the following sections of this chapter, we offer with confidence a theological dimension to the understanding of energy in relation, counterbalancing tendencies in society to create a divide between a linear, simplistic notion of power and an utterly chaotic false alternative.

Energy dynamically ordered

When a virtue is made of the absence of passion, life between people and in organizations and churches is devoid of energy and like the dead walking. Richard Rohr, in workshops on spiritual development, evokes the lost spirit in contemporary men; he describes this absence as an unlit fire, a characteristic of the age and a determining influence on organizations largely run dogmatically and unemotionally by men or on male-directed lines, often functioning with head and heart almost completely separated (Rohr and Martos, 1996, p. 21).

The renewed practice of Christian liturgy, influenced by an uneven but emerging feminine power in the Church, is only just recovering from the notion that no expression of personality or excitement is welcome if God's life is to be communicated. Spiritual guides such as O'Murchu and Cotter emphasize that justice and peace are not created simply through intellect and planning, but as an echo of God's personal relational life of friendship. Western European and North American debates about the present and future of human action and organization, including the Church, have lived within damaging false dichotomies. Simple solutions that ignore the complexity of situations are contrasted with unaligned and irrational chaos.

No single extreme approach or language is complex enough to describe the universe and God's dynamic life. This is not to capitulate to utter chaos, nor to latch on to a narrowly confined foundational explanation from which everything else can be explicated along a utopian linear track. An ordered freedom or constrained generativity can occupy the space between totalitarianism and chaos. The combining of the two polarities leads to a third notion, of complex ordering, disciplined freedom or passionate relating, that is neither utterly formless nor immaculately pure. Our proposal is that to become fully human and to reach a mature comprehension of matter is to accept the invitation to live with ambivalence. This is to choose to live out of the difficult but rewarding discipline that responds to God by becoming part of an intersubjective, dynamic, interactive energetic ordering that is at different moments turbulent, surprising, disturbing, agonizing, intense, joyful and deeply still.

Indeed, current trends in leading theories in fundamental physics, cosmology and computing sciences concentrate on a holistic approach to theorizing about the ordering of matter, rather than the inherited assumption that science, unaided, can explain everything. The late theoretical physicist David Bohm developed a theory of the universe as a flowing and unbroken wholeness in which process, flux and change are fundamental in an 'implicate (or enfolded) order' (Morgan, 1997, pp. 251–2). A conceptual upheaval ('chaoplexity', Keller, 2003, p. 188) designates matter not as normally orderly, stable and equilibrate, but as seething and bubbling with change, randomness and process. The indications are that the life of the world is best described in terms of a journey leading from a static state of being to a dynamic condition of becoming. The future is wide and opening; it 'cannot be predicted in detail from the past, either in principle or in practice' (Barbour, 1990, p. 220).

Increasingly theologians, in varieties of language and thought forms, are proposing an understanding of existence in terms of an intrinsic energetic relationality, echoing the God of hope, who in scripture is often characterized unpredictably as doing a new thing or the impossible. Daniel Hardy, for example, referring to 1 Corinthians 2.9–10, writes of the gift of life in the searching of God by the Spirit, not as fixed but as the implicit and dynamic energy, order and abundance of God (Hardy, 1996, p. 148).

In the search to find inspiration for the Church to contribute to the work of the world, power as energy in relation, an ontology of relationality offers one of the most creative contemporary theological resources. As Jesus, the Spirit and the Father are different but dynamically one, so no thing and no one exists apart from its relation to others. The principle of non-identical repetition means that no situation is exactly repeated. For good or ill every action has its effect on another; the life of one location affects life in another. However, the mere fact of relationship is of no significance in itself, as though to make a world of an easy-going, pain-free, amorphous haze. What is at issue is the particular character of the quality of relating, and for whom it provides nurture or improves the quality of living.

A theology of becoming

Questioning traditional theological categories and symbols of God is a vital part of the Church's mission and evangelism. This is in recognition of the many-layered power of religion, and Christianity in particular, in centuries of shaping human beings and society. A significant example is that of the nature of personhood and the quality of relationship between people. Christian symbols of God have exercised very significant power in shaping social, political and personal living. To fulfil its redemptive role and be a source of genuine freedom, Christian theology and practice have to address destructive concepts and patterns of power inherent in the life of churches before making claims to be able to open up new possibilities for others and make a different world achievable.

Another issue is that of suffering. Scripture offers us both the image of a potter with clay and that of parent with child. When Christians pray 'Almighty God' and exemplify forms of social and political structures that limit human responsibility, an ideal is presented of a perfect, all-powerful and dispossessing father. Questions arise: how would an all-powerful parent allow children to play in a world full of agony? if God is not omnipotent surely he must be impotent? is there a true place to stand beyond the dichotomy of a simplistic response or of one that allows no constraint to chaos? Some early Christian theologians opposed the Gnostic understanding that all creation is evil and to be avoided and rejected. Platonism and mainstream classical Greek influence on Christianity fostered the view that creation came from nothing and that the all-powerful, transcendent God neither needs, nor is in, this world. To show God as all-powerful and timeless, orthodox Jewish, Christian and Muslim theologians have long argued the case for creation *ex nihilo*. After all, if the Lord God is truly in charge, as the protagonist of this cosmic drama, why should 'He' be troubled by an 'Other'?

From Irenaeus, Bishop of Lyons, and by the time of Athanasius who in the fourth century shaped the Nicene Creed, Christian theology loses its roots in the God of Judaism who walks and struggles with the people. Instead it becomes associated with a simplistic form of Hellenistic dualism, rooted in the changeless, unmoved eternity of God and the unchangeable mess of the material world. Our inheritance is the traditional, stable Christian understanding of creation and salvation history, loathing heretical chaos and travelling from a simple beginning to its ultimate goal. God, who is totally in charge, in whom intelligent people may put their trust and to whom all should be grateful, is a wise, changeless, rational and timeless monarch. This common-sense theological approach to creation was rooted in the utter power of a Creator who is self-sufficient and to whom everything must succumb. Its pervasive effect on modern Western thought patterns is demonstrated in the polarization of the certainties of dominating power and terrifying alternative deep, dark chaos. It has left no room except for a dominating, manly, monotheistic and straightforward, nononsense understanding of energy, movement, human relations and the 'using' of passive people and the gaining of territory. The ordinary, broken, neighbourly and particular detail of a fragile people and world is swallowed up in disconnected glory.

A theology and practice of church for today will move away from a yearning for homogeneous, simplistic ordering, to embrace God's energetic, mutual, transformative life as creative multiplicity. Taking the example of jazz as an open form of musical improvisation, Jeremy Begbie argues for the abandonment of a mere dualism between order and absence of order. Instead of dualistic hierarchy, the interplay and mutual enhancement between order and chaos, as between Word and Spirit, produces a liberating engagement of constraint and freedom (Begbie, 2000, p. 187). Freedom and constraint are not necessarily opposites; freedom is not identical with the absence of boundaries but with the particular kind of energetic ordering that is mutual love, coalition, living with integrity, tending the universe, taking infinite care of our particular locality, as early signs of God's final ordering.

A growing desire to experience the particular energy of women, children, imagination, play, holistic patterns, depth, mystery, uncertainty and to undo all false dualisms is bedevilled still by a refusal to recognize the fluctuating deep as part of God's good creation. In this light the present struggles of society and the churches with those labelled lesbian, gay or bisexual are inevitable. The development of a theology rooted in the relational life of the triune God is a vital key to sharing in God's mission to repair a world that is increasingly polarized between the exercise of dominating control and unconstrained freedom from responsibility and tradition.

What is needed is an end to the belief in a God who created out of nothing. A theology of God enfolded with the study of the dynamic energy of the cosmos offers an alternative view of power that transcends the two polarities of making and letting be. One innovative approach to this task interweaves a mystical Jewish reading of the creation narrative of Genesis 1 as a densely layered movement of energy with recent developments in chaos theory that describe life in terms of non-linear, self-organizing complexities. Unlike the classical theism that still charges the Church's thought and practice, the author of Genesis saw no conflict between the possibility that the universe was created from a primal chaos and the power of God.

Keller links a key principle of chaos theory, 'extreme sensitivity to initial conditions', with a close hermeneutical study of the opening verses of Genesis. 'The butterfly effect of chaos theory intercalates its oscillations with the fluttering of the mother dove or brooding water bird – as also with the inter-discipline of theology and science' (Keller, 2003, p. 5). Critically engaging history and scripture in a project of constructive theology, she proposes a controversial translation of Genesis 1.1–3 so as to recover a fullness of energetic creating that historically the Church has often airbrushed out:

When Elohim began to create heaven and earth,
– at which time the earth was *tohu va bohu* (formless void), darkness was on the face of *tehom* (the deep), and the *ruach elohim* (Spirit of God) was moving upon the face of the *mahim* (waters) . . .
– then God said, 'Let there be light . . .' (ibid., p. 114)

Keller's innovative reinterpretation of the Genesis 1 account – an account frequently opposed by other scholars – jettisons the classical view of Creation in favour of 'terse triune chaos' (ibid., p. 267 n. 42). She proposes that, rather than being the object of the Creator God, the result of a one-off burst of energy, Creation mysteriously and constantly vibrates and trembles in maturing complex relation with Elohim. The nuances of the textual argument need not be rehearsed here (ibid, p. 114). Controversially but with increasing numbers of adherents, Keller perceives the first verse of Genesis 1 as a subordinate clause, the second as a parenthesis and only the third as the independent clause. It is a development of the translation of the eleventh-century French biblical and Talmudic interpreter Rashi, 'At the beginning of the Creation of heaven and earth when the earth was without form and void and there was darkness . . . God said, Let there be . . .' (ibid., p. 9).

Two important points are to be noticed. The first is that Creation is formed from chaotic matter. The second is the deconstruction of the classical linear, step-by-step view of Creation. Instead of the received dualism between a clinically God-designed Creation and chaotic nothingness, the way is opened to a third and turbulent possibility that is 'genesis'.

Deconstructing classical dualisms in preference for the 'interfluencies' of a bottomless deep, Keller develops a conception of divine order as open, changing, relational, offering the potential for every 'becoming' (ibid., p. 13), the human person fully alive.

Structured freedom, neither simplistically linear nor utterly chaotic, opens up a startling array of possibilities for life grounded in commitment to the God who is unity in relation. Discerning this tension between freedom and constraint lies, moment by moment, at the heart of all creativity. An artist having chosen a medium has taken on certain constraints to free creativity; a composer having chosen to write music for a particular instrument or occasion has accepted a particular rather than a vague creative medium. Marriage, the development of small Christian groups or the religious life combine the two interwoven values of commitment and freedom. A disciplined commitment is made to respect these particular unique people over time in the limitations and opportunities of particular circumstances, as a participation now in the messianic life of Christ. Christian faith itself as a communal space or climate depends on a freely accepted self-limitation as a path to a horizon otherwise inaccessible. Finding hope for the Church and the world requires that we dare to imagine how human energy can be expended in ways that value and celebrate – rather than fear and deny – the other, whether in ethnic difference, physical or mental agility, gender, culture, age or class. So, for example, instead of polarizing an 'objective' and a 'feeling' approach to issues and problems, we see the need to consider people and created life as held together in circles or fields of relating. This divine *koinonia* and trinitarian patterning in which God chooses to be bound to humanity in love, seems more likely to allow the strength and wisdom of each part to contribute to the flourishing and expansion of the whole. Love and friendship are practices and attitudes to be learnt from God, who is communion, in order to bypass familiar adversarial opposites.

Timothy Jenkins' work in the field of social anthropology contributes significantly to a recognition that truths emerge culturally rooted, not as universal ideals (Jenkins, 1999). Perceiving cannot happen at the universal level as our understanding is linked to particular encounters to which we are uniquely present (Irigaray, 2000,

p. 48). Daniel Goleman (1996) has inspired couples, families, hospitals, schools and businesses to consider relearning intimacy as the key to reducing stress, building motivation and collaborating effectively. Alyda Faber proposes the possibilities emerging for theological discourse through discovering meaning in the wisdom of 'labyrinthine flesh and spirit' (Faber, 2004, p. 320). Instead of a rational objectivity on the one hand and an uncontrolled rush of violent chaos on the other, the stability, resilience and volatility of bodies may be brought into play to remind us that all truth is limited and enriched by a particular perspective.

A theological rediscovery of Eros, liberated from narrowly genital connections, has the potential to challenge and help reconfigure the unsatisfying commercialized, male-dominated, defective world (Moltmann-Wendel, 2000). Unlearning the fear of joy, satisfaction, creativity and self-fulfilment is part of the task of a Church commissioned to demonstrate the communication of God in Jesus Christ. Notably, Audre Lorde seeks to rescue the 'erotic' from patriarchal trivialization, as a way of releasing energy by replacing with an awareness of deep internal knowledge the lethargy and lack of focus that characterizes so much of contemporary living. Recognizing how, in racist and patriarchal societies, bodies and the social meanings we attach to them give and receive violence, often of a sexual character, Carter Heyward offers the contrasts of the relationality of sensuality and intimacy. She identifies the 'perversion' of sexual energy when experienced and spoken of as violent boundary invasion and a travesty of erotic power. She is here contrasting 'the praxis of death' in contemporary society (e.g. in sadomasochism and pornography) with 'erotic power' that is moral good and the love of God and power in right relation (Heyward, 1989, pp. 3, 124).

Finding a way to heal broken power relations through conceiving the energetic life force of erotic power in mutual relation, offers alternatives to the increasingly familiar perversion of power relations and social structures of alienation. The Church's task becomes that of being an agent for creating goodness, energizing justice, indeed being a physical embodiment of God's love in a holistic experience of ourselves (Faber, 2004, p. 322; Stuart, 2003, p. 51).

An elusive Eros suggests the possibility of communities characterized by 'power-in-right-relation' and empathy with another, rather than by violence and avoidance of intimacy. This is that daring hope of the redemptive activity of God in Christ that overcomes the negative expectation of death to restore Creation's shape and reconcile all things in heaven and earth. Although pragmatically there is an all too common experience that sexual relations are abusive or turned to perversion, the aspiration for powerful, healing experience, joy, deep sexual connection, and passionate opposition to injustice offers a renewed expression of Jesus' gift of God's blessing or 'life in all its fullness'. The turning point of Carter Heyward's theology is the replacement of institutionalized, learned violence with an energy that is mutual and contains the seed of a new quality of human authority (Faber, 2004, p. 323). The contribution of gospel community practice to the world seeking peaceful words and actions to live within may, then, be that God's energy is revealed when our self and others are at their most flourishing in intensity with unabated yearning for what is true and good, 'a sensual guide to what is moral in life' (ibid.) rather than the adversarial politics of violence and self-seeking (Heyward, 1989, p. 93).

Vitally, Heyward constructs a theology of right relation rooted in an alternative understanding of authority to that which has long influenced Christian practice. Despite the ongoing resurgence of the idea of erotic energy in the language of spirituality, offered notably by Jim Cotter and William Johnston, Christianity has so often eschewed this notion in the name of purity or because its potential is to be too closely associated with abusive power. Indeed the ideas described here are certainly not without their challengers (Stuart, 2003, p. 55). Kathleen Sands has challenged the extended use of the metaphor of erotic power, noting the tragedy that often accompanies the full expression of the force of Eros (Faber, 2004, p. 327). The worldwide prevalence of AIDS and the use of rape as a means of warfare are stark reminders of the wounds inflicted on women, children and men in the pursuit of domination and repressed forms of relating. Critically, what is emerging is the need to uncover the Church's long history of dis-ease with sexuality, with its concomitant history of patriarchal domination and the threatening distortion of gender roles.

The American theologian Rita Nakashima Brock has tackled this dilemma through a re-visioning of the Christian doctrine of original sin. She explores this as the invitation in all brokenness and damaged health to see the healing possibility of believing in the fullness and sustaining presence of original grace. Jesus cannot be thought of alone; he not only releases those he calls his friends but is himself freed by contact between close friends in 'the erotic power of mutuality, the fundamental power of being' (Moltmann-Wendel, 2000, p. 102).

This is a model for the Church and for all human relating. Rather than standing over another to listen, hear and support, a radical friendship invites our gentle brokenness to be available to the other. Human persons are formed and distorted through the depth or solidarity of their encounter. Notably, the patriarchal model misshapes in two particular ways: by living approximately with others but actually in dissociation and by fixing stereotypical gender roles. Dialoguing with object relations theory reveals how instead of living to their full capacity, many adults protect themselves from emotional trauma by developing a 'false self'. This unreal, selfish construct bases self-worth on cultural or group identification, preventing the whole person from real communication with others and from experiencing and living the love and freedom of God. As this is true for individuals, a similar position develops in churches shaped by formal, impersonal and unemotional passivity.

A key path to such emotional disability (an inability to express anger, vulnerability or grief) may be the result of parents, in a perversion of their power, shaping their children to disconnect from knowing or expressing emotion. Massive quantities of energy are lost as humans inhabit this false self, afraid to own ambivalent responses to people and situations. Reconnecting with 'erotic power', not to be confused merely with physical sexual expression, increases energy for integrating and connecting human living, guiding the search for justice and seeking the fullest possible life.

Allowing ourselves to know the energy of God that pumps through our hearts, breathes in our lungs, quickens in our speech and races through our limbs must surely be one of the fruits of God's Spirit working in people and communities. If churches cannot assist us to make contact with this we have to ask how they are disclosing the dynamic of God's power among them and for the world.

Unlocking this stiffness in us and in communities would be called by some 'conversion', allowing God's love to reign in the whole of our lives, in speech and action. The Church's power to attract by showing people the passionate story of Jesus cannot be unleashed through theories about mission, new patterns of ministry or renewed liturgical texts. What our society needs now is a Church open to God's Spirit, so that deep veins of patriarchal socializing that have led to inhibiting trauma and disconnectedness can be healed. This will be through courageous, self-forgetful alternative practices of becoming and relating that bring out the heart's true energy, irrigating the flesh (see Brock, 1988).

The Church has the gracious gift of God's life to realize this potential in every person, to generate the spontaneous energy to overcome the damage of previous false socialization and release people to goodness and happiness. Violence, paralysis and repression is the exact opposite of Eros; when erotic power is avoided or denied, life becomes fragmented as pain of body and psyche. The ocean can be a powerful metaphor for expressing the vast and deep, loving, divine possibilities of connection and the enormous creative power of restless energy. The sea becomes dangerous only when in imagination it represents chaotic and monstrous power, to be controlled at all costs.

We have identified the value of these *theological* perspectives for helping to deconstruct dominating notions of power in favour of patterns of power suffused with the dynamic energy of the God who is *koinonia*. What is of critical value for this study is the urgent call of Heyward, Brock and Keller, in their different and overlapping contributions, to regenerate values and practices of power that can overturn false and inhibited personalities separating and alienating human beings one from another. The subversive gift of gay and lesbian theologies to the latent Enlightenment habits and speech of the contemporary Church is the invitation to re-examine rigid and linear certainties about self-identity and personal relations, family, Church and society. Through greater self-awareness, tenderness and contact, reflection and changes in attitude and behaviour, each person can contribute to and benefit from this process. Jesus demonstrates and bestows God's energy and blessing for a restored humanity, inviting a wholehearted response. This task of finding *shalom*-shaped energetic patterns of living places all theologies, especially those that claim to liberate us, under critique in the search for the communal performance of love.

Although these women writers have largely become frustrated by institutional Christianity, we find their insights and concepts pivotal for the reconfiguring of power relations in churches, families, societies and the global community. Their prophetic anger with the Church, together with eschatological hope for persons and sociality, in fact link them with the long chain of those who have constantly reimagined God better to mediate hope in a distorted world. There can be no debate about good relations in power sharing that is not rooted in an eschatological ecclesiology, a Church working for the final purposes of the triune God. Jesus from the beginning of his public ministry drew around him teams of varying size to be 'salt of the earth', working together to make known God's reign. Discussion of corporate Christian discipleship cannot be separated from the messianic dream of God's project with the universe (God's Kingdom). This movement of faith is inherently public, communal, social and political, and urgent: 'The lion has roared; who will not fear? The Lord God has spoken; who can but prophesy?' (Amos 3.8).

The early Christian writer Tertullian exclaimed 'See how these Christians love one another' (*Apology*, 39). Jean Vanier, founder of L'Arche, the community of those with learning difficulties, has taught consistently that in community are discovered both our deepest wounds and the mystery of forgiveness. St Francis, through his relationships of vulnerability before God, his sisters and brothers, and the poorest, demonstrates in a particular way how choosing to be dynamically ordered in true Christian community offers a renewed knowledge of God's energetic life in the world. This ordering is not about preferences and dislikes, but rather 'leaving the dead to bury their dead' in following urgently the possibility of knowing deeply the fullest humanity in ourselves and in those to whom we are assigned. Suppose each person dares to face the general human truth that finding the deepest good in and for others, in mutual co-intending, is their main aim in life. Despite Christian faith and our greatest hopes and achievements, each person contributes to the pain, self-centredness and destructiveness of society and needs to accept as a matter of fact that we are in one way or another (not literally but metaphorically) 'recovering alcoholics'.

Francis encourages his companions in mutual openness and gentleness with one another's wounds, always admitting with joy his personal failure and weakness. He demonstrates in detail how to subvert any pretence at superior goodness or discipline, urging leaders to show special love to those who are vulnerable to their weakness (Kirkpatrick, Doherty and O'Flynn, 2002).

Part of the Church's share in God's mission is to dare to expect this vibrant hope of an alternative pattern of energy, rooted in mutuality and the search for justice, to be born in ourselves and our church community. We the authors know well enough how difficult it is to stop relying only on the way of intellect, certainty, appearance, success, niceness and classical impassibility. We have in small ways also begun to sense the loss when we fail to trust that God can be present in failure, anguish, uncertainty, involvement, commitment, play, relating and vulnerability. We believe that in the writers with whom we have engaged here, in some of the people we know and trust in family and work, and in some of our own experiences we have dared to glimpse the potential of living in the divine energy given through the Spirit by the Crucified and Risen One.

3 | **Capability**

Sharing in God's power

An emerging theme so far has been the urgent and difficult call for the Christian community to know its power to help the world move on from old ways of thought and behaviour and to create new 'mental maps' (Isherwood, 2001, p. 96). Action focused on specific change has been a powerful concept for organizations since the early 1990s. 'Empowerment' and 'development' became buzz words as hosts of management theories and tools were developed. Individuals were encouraged to 'come out of their prisons' and take power in their lives; organizations developed notions of downsizing, re-engineering, leaner management, and outsourcing (Kinlaw, 1995). Within this movement the organizational consultant Dennis C. Kinlaw writes of three characteristics of capable people. They (1) have the relevant technical knowledge and skill for participation, making 'useful' decisions in problem solving and innovation; they (2) can match their knowledge and skill to an appropriate 'outcome'; and they (3) have necessary skills to influence and convince others. Feedback, performance connections, teamwork, and learning make for effective, empowered strategy. Developing the capability of organizations to deliver their product effectively, ethically and consistently, in a highly competitive market, became a primary theme in personnel and organizational growth. The organization's healthy development was seen to have benefits for the employee in experiencing empowerment and fulfilment. At all costs, failure was to be eliminated and problems fixed.

This rhetoric was a marked improvement on the assumptions of previous eras that management would use and control people to achieve its ends. However, the pressure not to fail continues to take its toll on the lives of individuals, families and society. Vigorous debate continues as to how far the Church should regard its work as likely to benefit from organizational and management theories and practices. The 'McDonaldization of the Church' (Drane, 2000) has unfortunately become a slogan by which to denigrate attempts to achieve greater efficiency, calculability, control and expected outcomes, supposedly at the expense of core values of respect, love and freedom. Drane expects the Church to find itself by losing itself in and for God, not by chasing numerical growth through goal setting and organizational formulae but by being re-energized by Resurrection power. So dance, prayerful searching, meeting people's real needs, and expecting conversion and wonder are the means by which he expects the Church to know its capability in society (ibid.).

Assisted by theologians who have lately rediscovered the relational power at the heart of God's work in creation, we have been exploring how to be freed from a choice between total constraint and open chaos. Elizabeth Johnson, with her Spirit-laden trinitarian understanding, speaks for women's interpreted experience and, like Zizioulas, talks of God's power in terms of mutual relations or communion. Against the grief and degradation of so much human experience, the Christian community can invite people to know God's struggle to bring to birth a new heaven and new earth (Isaiah 42.14). Furthermore, God's intense, active involvement in bringing Creation to fulfilment awakens our knowledge that God is the source of our deepest capability. Recognizing and embracing our own power, and therefore our joyful responsibility for contributing to the flourishing of the networks of families, neighbourhoods, schools, churches, society and the world, can be very demanding. As we have already explored, it begins with the tough realism that we often fail even to want to take our proper place. Indeed it seems increasingly difficult for people in these situations to acknowledge the existence of their power and capability to build up or break down relationships. So the work of parenting, community leadership, local politics, church development and global practice is diminished through a lack of personal and organizational nerve. Christian faith is, above all, a living process, rooted in the gospel, that practises worship, discipline, forgiveness and mutual compassion by particular groups of people who intend to be an advance sign of God's coming reign. Following Origen, in the late fourth century, we may speak of the Church's witness (separate from but always engaged with other communities) as the work of a people who know they are charged with a unique and critical task in society to show how life can be when grounded in the truth known in God.

The human spirit and all creation derive from the energetic power of the Trinity, a power informed by God's Word.

In Psalm 33, obedience to God's Word is a cause for happiness and the singing of God's praises. St Francis demonstrated the dangerous but blessed fruits of a radical and simple following of scripture as discerning God's will. In the 1970s in Latin America, liberation theology was born as embodied practice arising from groups of people who allowed scripture to address the world and its power relationships. The deeply subversive nature of this personal and intellectual movement is revealed in the opposition to it of conservative elements within the Church and by the torture and murders that often arose among those who perceived the threat to their reality in this way of being church and doing theology. Liberation theology did not begin with concepts or arguments but found its principle and foundation in the reality faced by the poorest and those pushed to the edge by wealthy countries and organizations. For Gutiérrez and others, the starting point for hope and new growth in church and theology was to recognize the will of the mysterious God in the face of millions of people who merely existed in dehumanizing conditions of deprivation. The poorest were evangelizing the world by breaking in to those living at ease and demanding that, in their poverty, they might see Christ crucified and respond. Following in the steps of Karl Barth, Ched Myers' political exegesis of Mark's Gospel makes passionate connections between the Word of God and the activities of the authoritarian powers of this world. For example, filled with compassion Jesus reminds us of the power of touch and, provoked by the leper to break convention, reaches out to the unclean (thus making himself unclean), both healing and cleansing him from social ostracism. Jesus then sends the leper to the priests (the legitimate authority) as a sign that gospel power, greater than that of any religious establishment, has been released. Mark repeatedly illustrates the new economy of God's powerful Word that brings radical hope to the violent world. The Old Testament witnesses to the Word of God (*logos*) as acting decisively for transforming, intruding and inverting. Israel's testimony to Yahweh is that God's utterance brings incomparable changes for good (Brueggemann, 1997, ch. 3). Yahweh through speech creates the natural world and a people to be in special relationship, to whom he makes promises. Yahweh promises on oath to be faithful to Israel in blessing successive generations. So a people of expectation and hope is created, delivered time and again from evil. Yahweh also commands Israel in full expectation that obedience will be returned, setting bounds to their activity and establishing an expectation that they act towards one another with a justice that reflects Yahweh's holiness. When Yahweh speaks, the expectation is that Israel will follow, especially through the transformational experience of the wilderness.

As we concluded at the end of Chapter 1, any organization, not least the Church, aims to be structured to demonstrate its deepest meaning. Worship, ethics and purpose form a threefold cord for Christian community that struggles persistently to know, transmit and lead the movement for God's truth in the disorder of the world. As we have seen earlier, the Holy Spirit assists the Church, through praise and communal forms of dynamic living, to participate in the movement of God's life in the world. The deep, open engagement of people with one another, revealed in Jesus of Nazareth and stirred by the Spirit, has been a recurring theme in our exploration of reordering the world according to the movement among us of the triune God. Through the interwoven practices and relationships by which we make sense of our life together we interact dynamically, finding and folding purposeful and effective societies around ourselves (see Hardy, 2001, pp. 238ff).

So a school or hospital, in the manner in which it treats staff, patients, pupils, visitors, its ways of learning and teaching, administration or dealing with crises, will perform or actively demonstrate its working values and beliefs. Christians who regard their business as their vocation can say 'What I do has meaning' (Childs, 1995, p. 1). This requires active boundary living, an alert balancing on the cusp of possibilities, success or failure. Many small deaths for individuals and communities move us forward through important and necessary changes. Churches and neighbourhoods reveal their intuitive awareness of this through the planning and performance of funerals and of other 'liturgical' events that make meaning where there is loss of hope or the tragedy of despair, as well as the celebration of creativity and joy (Ward and Wild, 1995). To be truly capable, an organization has to be in the constant process of knowing the meaning of its work. In dialogue with contemporary theories of meaning, especially the widespread repudiation of religious faith, Graham Hughes explores Christian worship as a dramatic way of making meaning of life. He proposes that the making of meaning is a combination of construction and discovery. So, inhabiting and performing our deepest meaning lies at the heart of human capability. As a sign of this possibility, to find and enact the meaning it recognizes in the triune God is the Church's task and the vocation the faithful God gives it the capacity to fulfil. This is not a work of easy complacency. Rather in a state of flux, creating worship is a paradigm of all living, as daring adventures and relationships that are 'daunting-but-thrilling':

> Perhaps a first requirement is that those who have had general and specific responsibilities for the planning and execution of the event (those who devised the liturgy originally, those responsible for the worship space, the priest or minister, other leaders, the musicians) will have absorbed deeply into themselves an awareness that the work in which they are engaged *is* a 'boundary' or 'liminal' (threshold) event; that it takes place at a kind of virtual 'edge' of what we can manage conceptually and emotionally; that the event is nullified if it is permitted (as it threatens constantly to do) to fall back into domesticity or 'routinization'. (Hughes, 2003, p. 301)

Learning to become real

Being successful is equated with being valuable, the opposite of being a worthless nobody. Fear of failure or of seeming foolish severely limits our capability. To pretend to ourselves or our friends and colleagues that we don't make mistakes, or to refuse to be in touch with our feelings, living merely on the surface, is a very common feature of our society. This natural human trait is a false security that diminishes what we can create.

> Now. When I have overcome my fears – of others, of myself, of the underlying darkness:
> at the frontier of the unheard-of.
> Here ends the known. But, from a source beyond it,
> something fills my being with its possibilities.
>
> (Hammarskjöld, 1964, p. 77)

When Jesus tells his disciples we must die to self he invites us to let go of a false and protected self, of being self-centred, in order to know ourselves transformed as increasingly we allow God to be at our centre. Echoing Paul's invitation to us to be in Christ and therefore in God, St Irenaeus notably proclaimed, 'The glory of God is the person fully alive.' Contemporary writers on organization and leadership emphasize the need for character, faith, an awakened soul, passion, a concern for others, and a secure sense of revitalized and responsible self (Cammock, 2003, p. 143).

To be lacking in self-worth or true connectedness with our own power is to be deficient in identity and integrity. Commitment to having a secure sense of self, really 'being there' in relationships and organizations, is deeply challenging as it means we face the possibility both of failing and succeeding, as well as learning to live with the ambivalence that, day by day, we shall be a mixture of success and failure. The natural temptation is to disguise our passion and to settle for stale, uncharged, unaware, objective fraudulence. This is a challenge especially for professionals when the temptation is to withdraw from real contact and hide behind the role of lawyer, military officer, priest, doctor or social worker. An evocative example of this set of choices as it affects the teaching profession, presented by educationalist Parker J. Palmer in *The Courage to Teach*, has, we believe, relevance for many others. His passion for educational reform centres on the challenge to schools and colleges to have the values of a movement rather than an organization. Palmer associates organizational approaches to education with being so focused on effective structures, economics and appearance that humane and mature possibilities in educational methodology are lost. He invites those who teach and their administrative structures to be 'divided no more'. For the sake of 'great things', which we would call the 'reign of God', Palmer believes educational communities should be characterized by values that release real humanity in the classroom:

1 *Diversity* – diverse viewpoints are demanded by the manifold mysteries of great things.
2 *Ambiguity* – we understand the inadequacy of our concepts to embrace the vastness of great things.
3 *Creative conflict* – conflict is required to correct our biases and prejudices about the nature of great things.
4 *Honesty* – to lie about what we have seen would be to betray the truth of great things.
5 *Humility* – humility is the only lens through which great things

can be seen – and once we have seen them, humility is the only posture possible.

6   *Freedom* – tyranny in any form can be overcome only by invoking the grace of great things. (Palmer, 1998, pp. 107–8)

Palmer's thesis is that it is impossible for educational institutions to deliver imaginative, honest, and questioning processes for transformative learning when, deliberately or unconsciously, they are living from an opposing set of imperatives for organizational success. There are of course clear parallels here for leaders with churches, and other organizations, tempted to offer superficial and compliant education that is not transformative for the whole person or institution. In all of these arenas, those who push the possibilities for increased liveliness, diversity, conflict and learning that demands a breakthrough between role and the human person, instead of being treated as pioneers and adding crucial value may instead find they have damaged their career, attracted punishment or professional exclusion, both emotional and physical. Palmer reports the subversive conversations after one workshop when teachers privately agreed with his notions of educational reform but could not say so publicly for fear of reaction from the established authorities. The integrity sought by this educational movement is rooted in daring to be true, with open heart and mind. Why should this be so difficult or unusual in the practice of learning? The invitation to all concerned with learning is to combine professionalism with human honesty.

Churches struggling with anxiety about their future demonstrate similar inner conflicts. A variety of understandings and perceptions of reality and vision will be held in a diocese, for example. Movements for change may well be attacked as destabilizing the safe path of inherited practice. Living with anxiety and holding liminality is extremely demanding. A natural splitting can lead to polarized positions either of 'grandiose' complacency with the way things 'are and should remain' or an overanxious or depressed sense that nothing is working and termination is in sight. The task of leaders to identify the vision and pastorally but firmly facilitate the painful process of change is crucial. In the software industry, while some agencies seek proprietary control, others deliberately encourage free access to the development of emerging patterns. Whereas some church leaders act as though they had a monopoly on social forms of the gospel and act as if the Church were a mechanistic religious system of control, in truth the Church that echoes God's trinitarian living operates on power that is 'not held but transferred to others with whom it is shared' (Hardy, 2001, p. 257).

As we saw in Chapter 2 when exploring erotic power as an antidote to patterns of domination, true good, the meaning found in the trinitarian God, is emergent from deeply mutual relationship. The poet Rumi says, 'If you are here unfaithfully with us, you're causing terrible damage'.

Knowing our true self

Palmer's exploration of the inner landscape of teaching is an excellent example of how the supposed capability of an organization can be eroded through lack of self-belief. Theologically, this is to overlook the raw, dynamic energy that exists with and between human beings as the power of God that bursts out to transform life's possibilities.

Expecting and calling into being communities that work with integrity is the work of a true leader. Being on the path to finding a secure sense of self is an essential element in developing as a leader in industry or the Church, a factor often overlooked in training programmes that overbalance towards the accumulation of new operational skills. A secure person will learn to self-reflect and consider criticism in a balanced way. Similarly, those who currently work to help men rediscover their spirituality and proper assertive roles as husbands, lovers, parents and members of society, emphasize the need for an inner authority for the sake of others. This is not the same as a heroic, controlling, authoritarian or macho confidence, but the result of urgently and consistently developing an inner, reflective life to minimize the wounding of successive generations.

We live in a hard-working, success-driven culture. However, even our strengths can become failures if we assume we can function in similar ways in every situation. The Church often forgets that to learn from failure and be accepted in less than perfection is the way offered by God. The notion of heroes of the faith promoted in the hymns and Sunday school of past eras is questioned, for example, by careful study of the biblical accounts of Abraham's faith in God. This faith is in reality a gift that unfolds within his relationship with Yahweh. Paul cannot speak of Abraham as an exemplar of virtue or belief: his 'righteousness' is the result of believing in God's promise. Abraham's significance is precisely in knowing that he is 'secondary in relation to the God of promise who calls him out of nothing and makes him who he is' (cf. Romans 4.17). So Francis Watson (2004) helps us to recognize that in the life of faith, dedication and deeds of unwavering obedience are of less significance than knowing God's blessing as one whose sins are forgiven. Dismantling the heroic is a vital project in our era.

The Church has often been unhelpful here in presenting a demanding image of a God who expects and condemns our failure to reach the mark. A fuller understanding of the God of scripture includes strands that remind us of a faithful God who is kind, the observer of our hearts, and who seeks out our loneliest and hungriest places. This God meets us in our fear and mistrust – as one who shares the journey, challenging, pursuing, giving with an abundance we can hardly begin to imagine. Through prayer, worship, reading and reflecting on scripture, the disciple may come to a proper self-love through the deepening awareness of God's love. Confident in this love, we may dare to leave behind the protections and masks through which we either despise ourselves or defend ourselves against every criticism. Either extreme is a negation of our true self, though it can be challenging truly to accept our self, recognizing our failures but not pretending to be without gifts.

The Congregations and Business Life Project finds that, increasingly, laity assert that their daily life is their Christian ministry and that making the connection is very significant (Childs, 1995, p. 6). From his personal experience in industry, Hugh recalls recruiting transport fitters: 'Tom, who had already been out of work for two years, when offered the job pointed out with some fear that he was already 59 and that we would only get another six years' work from him. Despite his courage and honesty, he had come to believe society's myth that his age had somehow removed his capability and seemed afraid that we might also discover the myth to be true. However, given the job, Tom became the most reliable of employees and would turn a hand to anything!'

Realistic recognition of our true capability is frequently damaged by an inability to achieve and, more particularly, by our willingness all too easily to submit or accept the lack of immediate success. Anyone who has served on a committee can recall the moan, 'It won't work: we tried this twenty years ago and it didn't work then.'

Something in our experience conditions us, having tried and not succeeded immediately, to be cautious of encountering the same pain again and to be afraid of having another go. Individually, this is an understandable reaction: being stung by nettles while clearing weeds, narrowly being missed by a car when crossing the road, or slipping on black ice makes us warier next time. This is the basis of learning and survival.

Creative organization

Churches frequently forget that their defining character and power derive from the presence of the crucified and risen Lord. In the Resurrection the nature of God's power and presence among us is recast. The Resurrection introduces the radical notion of forgiveness as a way of changing the whole of life. We are no longer bound to envy, to rivalry, to the keeping of old scores, to feeling a victim of circumstances. Jesus in the Gospel of John (chapters 8 and 9) shows that God has more problems with those who exclude sinners from the community than with the sin itself. The woman taken in adultery and the blind man healed in the Pool of Siloam are easily forgiven through faith in the God who raised Jesus from death. Subversively, Jesus' problem is with those who would throw out these people from their place in the community. According to the ethic of Jesus in the Gospels, sin is not so much to be found in the one excluded as in the act of exclusion by members of the community. The Pharisees become blinder through claiming to see more clearly. The Anglican theologian Alan Paton, in *Too Late the Phalarope*, allowed that an offender can be punished, 'But to punish and not restore – that is the greatest of all offenses. If a man takes unto himself God's right to punish, then he must also take upon himself God's promise to restore.'

South Africa's Truth and Reconciliation Commission (TRC) offered a bold step of faith by practising Christian belief in reconciliation. The world needs the particular resource of Christian faith in the pursuit of restored human interrelations and the transformation of society. It is best understood in terms of developing human sociality through encounter in which, by fully meeting the 'other' (neighbour or enemy), God challenges us to take responsibility for our contribution to building ethical and sustainable community (de Gruchy, 2002, p. 91).

The stories of unbearable suffering rehearsed to the Commission, combined with memories of so many other dehumanizing atrocities, forced Archbishop Tutu not to speak glibly about forgiveness and reconciliation. Though often despised for his apparent naïvety, he dared to hope, unsentimentally, for healing to emerge from the costly refusal to seek retribution from those who had so badly failed in their dealings with those who were different (Tutu, 1999). Organizations generally are coming to recognize that positive benefits can accrue not only when things go well but also when things fail: there are always lessons to be learnt and new levels of honesty and connection to be discovered. Many institutions recognize this intuitively and, just as individuals reflect on their own successes and failures, so organizations can learn from experience. No organization or society is frozen as its capability is built up through eras, through events, people and ideas. Through time, complex patterns grow or are layered through ways of relating and being with one another. This is the wisdom by which communities have the capacity to meet and respond to ruptures and dislocations within the environment.

A number of issues flow from this. Reflection shows how the culture of institutions can reduce the potential for maturity. Indications are that transparency and directness are rarely found within hierarchical organizations. Instead they promote a spirit of competitiveness and fear, combined with an atmosphere of secrecy and blame. Evidence of personal immaturity includes the adoption by those in charge of the behaviour of controlling parent and the avoidance of mutual relations as requiring too much vulnerability. Such phenomena militate against the essential conditions for the organization to flourish, such as willingness to learn and to promote a spirit of openness in all its people. The long hours and pressure, competing demands and fragmented work patterns of modern life require strategic counterbalance. Routines of quietness, meditation, individual and group therapy and journal writing are increasingly common among the younger generation of leaders and executives (Astley, 2002, pp. 82–3).

Whereas individuals may reflect in private, without others knowing their true contribution to success or failure, comparative reflection within an organization requires the positive expectation of public openness and honesty, not to mention personal courage. Where fear and blame rule, it will be very difficult to get people dispassionately to discuss the high and low points of their work or to reveal the places where they feel inadequate. This is hugely inhibiting to any organization that claims to want to learn from its experience. Tom Peters has studied the results of institutions and organizations with a low tolerance of failure. He lists alarming outcomes where a huge dread exists among employees of revealing even the tiniest of errors. Small failures are individually hidden and fester until they accumulate, causing big failures further down the line; small failures, since they are unacceptable, do not quickly lead to adjustments, but are followed by huge efforts to fit square pegs into round holes; data are faked or hidden, so that failures can be seen as successes or hidden from those in other functions who could help, because one boss doesn't want to lose face with their peers; those at the top are kept in the dark and misled if only by omission, and then commit themselves further and further on the basis of incorrect knowledge – making subsequent exposure of failure even harder; no learning takes place, especially among politicized seniors, because no failures ever come to the surface, and normal human give-and-take, chiding and crowing, is replaced by stilted posturing; real tests are delayed and delayed as more and more simulations are done, in a panicky, time-consuming effort to make sure that no failure occurs on the first test, one which will now be highly visible and expensive; and, finally, truth, fun and speed all go down the drain (Peters, 1988, p. 263).

> Secondly, and the corollary to this first point, is that an organization wishing to learn from past mistakes needs not only to encourage openness but has actively to encourage people to be prepared to make mistakes. 'Actively and publicly hail defiance of the rules, many of which you doubtless laboured mightily to construct in the first place.' (ibid., p. 263)

We may not learn only by our mistakes, but where individuals are actively encouraged to take considered risk significant gain is made. If we risk nothing we gain nothing. The whole Christian journey is based on the risk of faith; as Peter realized, however falteringly, we need to get out of the boat to walk on the water. The early Church had a sense of the dynamic power and awe with which each generation of Christians needs to make fresh contact. Worshipping Christians corporately encountering God's holiness are formed as the Church and called to show the same passionate love as the crucified

Christ. Indeed, the expectation that life will be comfortable, that we will face no risk, pain or difficulties, either as individuals or as a community, is to deny much of the central truth of our faith. Dietrich Bonhoeffer defines 'cheap grace' as

> the preaching of forgiveness without requiring repentance, baptism without Church discipline, Communion without confession, absolution without contrition. Cheap grace is grace without discipleship, grace without the cross, grace without Jesus Christ, living and incarnate. (Bonhoeffer, [1937] 1954, p. 38)

The Church's high-risk strategy is to introduce God's alternative ordering of power relations, a community that serves and takes to itself all who suffer or are forsaken. Its particular ordering is rooted in patterns of repentance, confession, contrition and absolution which all imply failure in some degree. Here we walk a tightrope between the Christian's aim to be Christ-like and a pragmatic recognition that the surest and firmest path to success is principally through our mistakes. Far from advocating that we should actively seek to make mistakes, we nevertheless recognize the command of Jesus to accept failure in ourselves and others. The ministry, death and resurrection of Jesus is a clear sign that the kingdom cannot be truly advanced without losing life. Passion is to risk being so overtaken with hope, with such commitment, that in every situation and in the whole of oneself, pain, disappointment and suffering are inevitable.

Even in organizations that have developed an open culture, if there is no systematic corporate approach to learning from experience, any learning will necessarily be restricted to particular individuals, who will themselves feel threatened by lack of systemic support. In this very common situation, the ability of organizations to build on past lessons depends entirely on the experience of those who are particularly self-reflective and insightful. Deeper and long-term learning through risk-taking is far better accepted into the life of organizations but time and again, lone prophetic figures are seemingly punished for their innovative viewpoints and willingness to experiment and inevitably cause a degree of chaos. Organizations that fail publicly to support their pioneers severely inhibit future development.

Capability grows through reflection on the past in the light of present demands. The rich history of printing, agriculture, education or music eloquently demonstrates how knowledge and experience are distilled from one generation to another. However, shared corporate experience (whether in business, government, charity or church) becomes a major and effective tool only when the organization chooses to capture and record the lessons it has learnt, sharing widely so that others may learn and build on experience. For the Church, tradition is just such a legacy, since much of what we understand is based on the learning and distilled wisdom of our forebears in faith.

The Church's witness in every age is formed by the past and yet also by its priorities now as it discerns how to witness to God's coming reign in any given set of circumstances. The debates and challenges of previous centuries certainly inform our present practice, yet in the power of the Holy Spirit, there can be nothing more crucial than how we are responding to God here and now.

Learning to be self-reflective

A vital element in human development is review. The leader's task is to monitor the overall performance of a team or teams to ensure they are open to improving the value of their 'product'. Appraising the entire system is a higher priority than checking how well individuals are performing. All activity is a function of the wider field, and creativity and growth will be occurring both at the boundary of the interface between teams or individuals and that of the entire organization. Changing the frame of reference, the culture and performance of the organization requires everyone to be helped, via a kind of ripple effect, to imagine how this organization could be and offer 'more'. So the ideal or reframed perception becomes possible through a common commitment and performance. The admiration, loyalty and recommendation of 'customers' resulting from permanent review is something that all participants in the organization can be encouraged to prefer, rather than ignoring dissatisfied customers and constantly chasing new ones. Changing the environment – like providing a health eco-system in a tank to promote reproduction in fish – can be just as vital as concentrating on the effectiveness of people. But satisfaction of the human desire to be energized and transformed can result when a company has a culture of high performance in which everyone perceives how their behaviour, sense of responsibility and willingness to cooperate across boundaries brings about a virtuous cycle of maximum value. (In this area Robin is indebted to Perception Dynamics Workshops (2005) for their research into systems thinking.)

This requires the honesty to recognize that the desire to succeed necessitates facing up to, and learning from, the opposite: success can only be achieved through repeated failure and introspection. In fact, success represents the 1 per cent of your work which results only from the 99 per cent that is failure (Soichiro Honda, founder of Honda Motors, quoted in Peters, 1988, p. 259).

Effective organizations recognize the learning opportunity non-success gives. Why were we there? What were we trying to do? What went well? What didn't? Could we have done it better? If we were doing this again, how would we approach it? Such reviews are not intended to blame. Indeed blame has no part in an effective review since this simply acts to reinforce feelings of failure and self-defence. Review, carried out in an open and positive way, particularly when facilitated by an impartial observer, creates opportunities to learn from our experience. Current literature on organization theory, related to the whole of life, carries many examples.

Stephen Covey, for instance, presents the intriguing possibility of a diary that is not merely reactive to the demands of others or to our own predilections. He describes how to keep a balanced but effective programme of work through identifying no more than seven roles (personal life, spouse/parent, and up to five projects at any one time). Within each role he suggests we identify no more than three current priorities to be worked out proactively in terms of daily appointments. Equally there is room for regular reflection as to which roles or goals are being marginalized or amplified and for what reasons (Covey, 1999). Similarly, 360 Degree Review expects employees to receive constructive criticism of their performance from working colleagues and subordinates as well as superiors. Current church leadership development programmes invite course participants to receive feedback from several among those who experience them as leaders: parishioners, clerical colleagues, area dean, churchwarden, organist, or local head teacher. Experience shows that such processes have their pitfalls and are open to abuse. Some guidance or training for those engaged in 360 Degree Review increases its potential benefit.

For Christian disciples, the Examen of Conscience is one form of review that enables a balanced consideration of the day's experience, reflective learning from it and, above all, consideration of where God was in the day just gone. It is rooted in God's gift of life and of the ceaseless invitation for us to 'put on Christ' by seeing our lives through the lens of our participation with the Trinity. Beginning with thanksgiving that everything has its origin in God (John 17.10) and for the gifts given to me, I am invited to ask how I was drawn to God today and learnt about God through ordinary things. In all the mixture of experiences did I allow God's word to come alive through prayer, scripture or liturgy? Have I been a sign of Christ's presence to others? In what ways did I reach out to those on the edge or to cooperate with God in the wider world? Where are the places in my life that are still resistant to God's love and in need of healing? Through a sense of grateful acceptance and the joy of being on the way to holiness, I can have hope for the future, 'racing for the finish, the prize to which God calls us upwards to receive in Christ Jesus' (Philippians 3.14).

The Examen is a positive expression of the invitation of Jesus to life in all its fullness. It offers a sense of learning and of growing closer to and recognizing God both at work and in the entire detail of our lives. Individual, regular personal review is an interior process, rooted in the unconditional love of God, that learns from experience, positive and negative, reapplying it in each new situation. Just as individuals learn, often subconsciously, from their experiences, so groups of people (organizations) may also learn, although the continued reapplication of such knowledge is harder to manage and achieve. Later in this chapter we describe the concept of the learning organization, derived from the work of Chris Argyris and Donald Schon with a view to showing how the individual approach of review may be harnessed and applied to a whole organization (Huczynski and Buchanan, 2001, pp. 127ff).

Nourishing the networks of society

Showing the world its true life, in the light of the knowledge of God, the local church has the task of facilitating the interweaving of Christian hope, theology in practice, in partnership with politicians, community workers, religious communities and financial supporters. As with individuals, society does not always recognize its own capability, either positive or negative. This is a particular testimony of social groups in inner cities, excluded from political and economic discourse in wider society. Duncan Forrester and Kenneth Leech are persistent examples of prophetic Christian voices concerned to draw attention to and bring about change in the power structures of urban poverty. They represent thousands of Christian disciples committed to 'wrestling with the interwoven forces that permanently bind so many human beings, distorting their character and leading to disabling self-hatred' (Forrester, 2001, p. 42).

Church community has to begin with itself if it is to fulfil its wider role. The Church enters most fully into its meaning as a sacrament of trinitarian relationality when it practises and works in society 'to effect and enjoy the relationality of difference' (Boff, 1988, pp. 236–7).

> Hugh describes the situation of a girl with Down's syndrome. Her parish priest had been persuading the congregation that every member had a part to play. At the end of the service the girl asked him what was her role. At first he was somewhat nonplussed, but eventually he said 'Your job is to welcome people,' for indeed she had that openness and capacity for love that most of us are afraid to show. From that day she welcomed every person who visited the church with an uninhibited hug and smile of welcome.

The Church's task is to encourage each individual to recognize their capacity to contribute something. Its power emerges through its presence being acknowledged, celebrated and put to work. Much hidden work, day by day, mobilizes webs of movements through parishes, boroughs, constituencies, across social and economic fault lines. The problem lies in convincing people that they are indeed capable, that they do have gifts, and then in injecting sufficient energy into what is often an apparently hopeless situation to create an acceptance that there is vital potential. The Church, precisely because of its loss of prestige, has the unique vocation and opportunity to build up hope in fragmented social networks.

In developmental work in dioceses and parishes it is striking how locked into constitutions, habits of mind and self-limitation we can choose to be. Some use religion as a chaplaincy to protect us from a rapidly changing world; others struggle against the tide of secularization to keep the church open, solvent and continuing to exist – keeping the rumour of God alive through familiar forms. The way of Jesus, exemplified so riotously by Francis, is to dare to exist only in defending the invisible poor on the edge of economic systems and in voicing a challenge to all dominating power that grinds people in the dust. A Church called to this vocation would itself choose poverty but its continued existence would not be an issue.

The evocation and encouragement of creative possibilities, amid situations of contingency and ambiguity, fosters a powerful sense of self-worth in people who can in turn change their world. To show that God's sociality is truly extended into relationship with everyday living, the Church, having relearned its own common life from the life of the Holy Trinity, has a key role in creating environments in which people come to value not merely their own gifts but those of the society in which they live. It is through such mutuality, participation and consultation that society becomes community in the equal dignity and different contributions of all. To work for sustainable and just living is to negotiate in active hope for transformed communities.

But the disempowerment of self-disbelief is not limited to the indigenous population. Many asylum seekers and economic migrants, often – or so it sometimes appears – publicly reviled and persecuted along with serial killers and paedophiles, arrive with considerable qualifications and experience in areas such as medicine and education, only to end up in unskilled, low-paid employment at the margins of the economy. While our society chooses to exercise its power (as authority) *over* these people, this does not mean that their power (as capability) is in any way diminished, although the situation in which they often find themselves might well lead them to believe it to be the case. Despite a sense of disenfranchisement, they still have capability despite being restricted in their ability to act. It is a loss to the whole community when an individual or a group of people are so far disabled from using their abilities and skills that they are not only unable to contribute in any meaningful way but more significantly lose belief in themselves and their capability. The greater publicity focused on such groups, and the prevention of people from working or making a contribution from their skills, makes it significantly harder now than ever before to handle the rejection that such disenfranchisement brings. A key factor in turning capability into successful action is to have a vision of what the future might be and an effective process for moving from the present condition to the desired state.

The world sustained in God's truth

We have repeatedly referred to the credibility gap between the Church's highest aspirations and its abject failure. Although the Church as organization palpably loses its authority and energy, God who never loses faith maintains it in its capability. Its chief resource is Christian faith itself, expressed and rediscovered through its collective wisdom and history, its tradition, its present structures and finances and, above all, its people. The Church's belief is that it is a sacrament of God's love for all creation. Church communities, properly motivated, envisioned and empowered are sustained in their capability to deliver, irrespective of whether or not we are able to measure the output. The outward current 'success' of churches, in terms of numbers or financial sustainability, is no true indication of the people's long-term faithfulness or the presence of the crucified Christ as a sign of how God has constituted the world. Fortunately our limited response cannot limit the ultimate success of God's creative project (Jeanrond, 1989, pp. 108–9).

Chapter 2 concluded that to respond authentically to God's movement of energy in the world is to accept the chaos, to grow in maturity rather than hiding behind a false self, and to commit ourselves as participants in the vulnerable but hope-filled project of drawing together a world of difference. The Church exists to show the world its true life, including how, despite all appearances (human need, global disintegration and evil), it is held in its long-term capability by a faithful God. As we have already argued, the communal practice of the gospel finds its distinctive meaning when it frees people to be fully themselves through relating deeply to the trinitarian God. Although we betray our trust and attempt to find security by holding on to the ephemera and paraphernalia of past expressions of faith, God, present in the Church, inscribes in us personally and corporately a kind of belonging that cannot be erased. We need to complement here the earlier discussion of vulnerable interweaving with the trust that God provides the necessary gifts for the Church to live the particular forms of social life that advance the triune God's work among us.

The tradition within which we, the authors, stand believes that, through the corporate practice of regular participation in the celebration of the eucharist, our lives are formed and maintained in a lifetime *habitus* of identity (Ford, 1999, ch. 6). This is not a form of neo-triumphalism. David Ford inspirationally describes the formation and sustaining of our eucharistic selves and communities as blessed, placed, timed and commanded. There are many other gifts and challenges we receive in eucharistic living, including the deep capability to become and do all that is required to be an anticipation of God's eschatological purposes.

Daniel W. Hardy unfolds this as the 'dramatic enactment of social meaning'. The mutual participants in the eucharistic enactment, joining past, present and future, share in God's final drawing together of the work of creation. However, as we discussed earlier, this is not based on infallible certainties. The in-folding of social meaning with the life of the Trinity is a struggle lived out in ambivalence and through constant repentance, reconciliation and new beginnings. In other words, the capability that God offers is within the chaos of everyday contingent living, in which 'human social meaning does not lose its character as fragile, incomplete and forward-moving even as it is drawn by God toward the eschatological finality of God's work' (Hardy, 2001, p. 246). A core element in the Jewish–Christian scriptures is the pronunciation of the world as 'good', created in the righteousness of God. Communal Christian celebration of the eucharist is the sacrament of God's energetic and Spirit-driven presence, maintaining the world and enabling its people to flourish.

The learning organization

The theory of the learning organization, in its aspirations and language, presents itself as an obvious dialogue partner in this search for the development of human capability. It believes in the innate power of people and networks to engage with their potential through the risky process of listening. In order for businesses to release their greatest potential there are good reasons to be concerned about an ethical position. Earlier we noted the move away from accepting the authenticity of a detached, rational-objective view of people and work. Experience and reflection indicate a growing recognition that reasoned argument alone is an inadequate basis for corporate living. This presents a profound moral question for commercial enterprise. Is it possible to be financially successful as well as actively promoting the well-being of people and the whole creation?

Whenever people come together to act as a corporation other people's ways of living will consequently be affected. As a conscious, corporate body with an identity, an organization is not free to operate in isolation, but interacts with other people and organizations in a global environment. Although the entrepreneurial focus demands both economic and human action, those who are the workers, through creating and observing morally responsible decisions, constantly create or deconstruct the authority of the organization and of themselves. The directors of an organization have begun to recognize that they have a decisive responsibility to ensure that, as an act of voluntary self-obligation, its actions and its treatment of workers are proactively ethical. The added value for the organization is an increase in its authority as developing a credible corporate identity. Senior staff, though taking the ethical lead, cannot achieve this alone. The authority of the organization in society will depend to a high degree on the motivation of all participants to be committed to the acting out of its corporate ethic, whether implied or consciously articulated.

The learning organization describes itself as facilitating the learning of all its members and consciously transforming itself and its context (Pedler, Burgoyne and Boydell, 1997, p. 3). Just as the identity of people is negotiated in the fact that they connect, listen to and engage with others and in the quality of that relationality in particular situations, so organizations develop as part of a greater whole and are shaped by their response to the wider environment with its variety of cultures and values. A deceptively simple example, with biblical precedent, is a practice that shows concern for others and builds trust and confidence, namely paying bills when they are due 'rather than doing business with other people's money' (Childs, 1995, p. 33).

The corporate ethic of the organization will develop in the balance it chooses between shaping itself internally and the degree to which it makes morally justified decisions, or not, in orientating itself to others in the course of its business transactions. The authority of the organization is determined largely by the response it makes to questions such as 'By what values will our total operation be guided?' Its identity and the quality of its work will be formed through the decisions it makes about norms of behaviour and the extent to which all the participants embrace and follow them through consistently. The autonomy to manage themselves in their own roles can only be real for a group of weavers or nurses if consequent changes are recognized and followed through for managerial roles elsewhere in the system (Miller, 1993, pp. 224, 231, 237). The powerful reputation of the organization is further enhanced through reinforcing employees in moral integrity by increasing resistance to corruption and criminal behaviour. Advantage comes to organizations, both commercial and voluntary, that have worked to build up the trust of being 'good enough', by honouring staff and being internally healthy (Kleinfield, 2000, p. 45).

Corporate ethics can bring great advantage to organizations provided that it transcends spin and superficial behaviour to arrive at a serious inner conviction consistently applied. An organization with integrity genuinely seeks the welfare and personal development of its employees, rather than seeing them merely as a means to create money for shareholders. The abuse of people, generally the main organizational asset, is counter-productive. A key element in the ethic of an organization will be the recognition and defence of the dignity and rights of each stakeholder involved. This responsibility, say for safety, comes before any cost–benefit considerations. The public outcry at the deaths of cockle-pickers in Morecambe Bay early in 2004 stands as testimony to this. Complexity arises when various sets of ethical principles conflict in a given context, such as when operating trans-nationally.

Research confirms that new forms of group working cannot successfully be transplanted without sufficient regard to the processes involved in earlier changes (Miller, 1993, p. 233). To succeed in the aim of such self-imposed aspirations to authenticity requires tough work at every point of scale within the company and leaves it vulnerably open to criticism when it under-performs. Nor can this kind of authority be achieved unless ethical principles are truly integrated into corporate values and held to through times of internal restructuring or changing external context. The learning organization looks for a completely new model beyond even the most efficient type of bureaucratic command-and-control. This model is represented by trees in which water, sap, life forces continually flow up from the ground, through the middle, outwards, downwards, back to the ground. Healthy companies are concerned not only about profit for shareholders but have recognized that the ground of their energy is in fact the shared identity of all the workforce, not as static but as a continual flow, producing networks and overlays of relationship and cooperation (Pedler, Burgoyne and Boydell, 1997, pp. 20–1).

The authority of organizations is best achieved when characteristics of community creation and cohesion, solidarity and loyalty are demonstrated, as 'human beings make meaning when they can go by something that corresponds to their real being, their dignity as persons, namely spiritual and ethical values' (Kleinfield, 2000, p. 48). Peter Senge, a leading exponent of learning organization practice, builds on Maslow's motivation theory which drew out a hierarchy of needs (see Chapter 2). Assuming that companies would be meeting the lower-order, 'basic' needs of workers, Senge looked for a mind shift that would aspire to meet the 'higher' needs of people. The qualities of leadership, integrating reason and intuition, required for this development, offer strong parallels with contemporary aspirations in building Christian community (Senge, 1990).

1 *Personal Mastery* involves self-development, 'continually clarifying and deepening our personal vision, of focusing our energies, of developing patience and of seeing reality objectively'. Christian discipleship, prayer, spiritual journeying, developing scriptural imagination immediately come to mind as distinctive Christian parallels. As in the Acts of the Apostles, Christian communities that choose to live intensely often discover a renewed coherence and energy, which in turn results in numerical growth and greater capability to act as Christ anointed in the Spirit.

2 *Sharing Mental Models* invites members of organizations to pool their collective and different perspectives for the creation of something more. A church might, for example, galvanize participants to share their faith stories, to discover true life, to work ecumenically, to enjoy the fruits of the entire Jewish and Christian tradition, to look to the worldwide Church and to be inclusive, and concurrently learn to be delighted by difference. To think of a local church as a community of wisdom is a reminder of those occasions when congregations come to new life through someone giving time and leadership to encourage

and support them in drawing together the strands of all that they know about God, in growing in friendship and mutual care, in respecting the growth and setbacks in others, in voicing doubts and uncertainties and in making a significant difference to the lives of others.

3   *Shared Vision* looks to everyone to be constantly moving beyond compliance, to be growing and learning out of a desire to develop. Churches that move beyond complacency expect Christians to be going deeper, exploring new patterns of worship, re-examining their belief, expecting God to be at work in their lives and in them in the world and to be using retreats, contemplation and the pursuit of justice as ways of growing in love. The Anglican Diocese of Monmouth in Wales, for example, has recognized that Christians need to be growing personally for the local church to have energy for responding to God's mission. Part of this is for each disciple to have a rule of life. Each person's rule will be different but will cover the whole range of discipleship. The encouragement of spiritual direction skills in many is a key element in this movement. For the Church the norm from which to develop its eschatological vision, as its particular contribution to transforming society, is the holiness of God, encountered especially in worship. Worship is the meltwater or the head of the spring of Christian faith and practice. Uniquely, liturgy and word are the way in which those who are in Christ cross the border into God's truth and love. The extraordinary and uniquely rich resource for the Church is the unbroken relationship between the practice of holiness, community (or sociality) and the praise of God (worship). Earlier we explored the profound contemporary moves towards a sense of self as essentially relational. The holiness of which we speak puts no distance between itself and ordinary living and working. A social holiness is the only kind there is: relational, complex, dynamic and performative. This spirituality is rooted in God who is not an inert, Platonic perfection, but in dynamic engagement with all creation. Worship is not the creation of the community so much as God's living energy making a community in which the members are simultaneously lifted into glory and into their responsibilities or vocations.

Experience of creative worship is not always easy to find. Examples are most frequently found at conferences, colleges, courses or retreats when the experimental can be expected and carefully planned. Local churches need liturgy planning groups that make time to be creative. Robin remembers co-planning the worship for a conference on mission in east London. A surprise element in shaping the empty room for the liturgy was the borough household rubbish collection. In the early morning the doorways of shops and warehouses contained an amazing variety of debris. The result was a hugely inconvenient cross covering the conference floor (over which everyone had to climb for three days) created from scrap metal and bricks. Yet, the connection between faith, worship and local life was tangible.

However, heaven comes Sunday by Sunday in a eucharistic celebration that connects some or all of the following: the readings announced in advance and read by many beforehand; care that the liturgical confession varies in form and that everyone is prepared to think about its significance for them well before the worship begins; hymns, psalms and songs carefully chosen to draw out the theme and to meet the needs of a range of people; the themes of the readings introduced and brought out throughout the service; a blend of silence, space, informality and time for all generations to speak; preaching that connects the situation of that community, the faith tradition, and is true communication; varieties of ways of sharing bread and wine. In short, worship that takes God's presence with utmost seriousness and joy and in infinite variety.

4   *Team Learning* assumes that workers are not random individuals but thoughtfully committed to one another in response to new possibilities. God's holiness is most aptly performed for the world through those developments 'capable of maintaining and directing in the inherent relationships of all people in all dimensions of life' (Hardy, 2001, p. 18). Churches rooted in the triune God, formed as communion and limbs of a single dynamic body, will be finding ways of growing together, listening to everyone, learning how to share a common purpose, to make decisions by negotiation and to offer genuine support to one

another without being inward-looking or divisive. In practice churches today draw up statements of purpose. An example from a parish in New Zealand says:

> We the people of St Andrew's, covenant this day to:
> - Affirm one another's ministries
> - Seek and welcome newcomers
> - Be open to the Holy Spirit among us
> - Celebrate God's goodness
> - Have fun together and
> - Be the Body of Christ in our community.
>
> (North New Brighton, Christchurch, New Zealand)

This was achieved through the work of the congregation over many months with the careful accompaniment of a diocesan-appointed enabler. The task of leaders in the Church is not to impose decisions, even after consultation, but to make a space in which everyone is heard so that there can be consensus around an emerging way forward. In such an approach great care needs to be taken to arrange meetings, physically and emotionally, so as to receive everyone's contribution. The one who chairs must listen deeply, constrain those who talk too much, draw out the quiet, expecting a fluid movement between seriousness and laughter, allowing for a respectful progress to a decision or policy. Looking for God to speak through surprising voices is an ingredient in practising the Good News in community. Prayer is the key. Direct speaking to God, linked with a scriptural passage, expecting God to act now makes for a vibrant church that refuses to be either defeated or grandiose.

5 *Systems Thinking* integrates the other disciplines so that the whole is seen in terms of all its parts together, for working with the patterns and relationships in the subtle interconnectedness of living systems. The authority of a church grows when it sees organic behaviour in worship, service, mission, learning and organization. It requires a shift of heart and mind in every participant, lay and ordained; it means that the local church as an expression of the entire Church (*koinonia*) never sees itself in isolation from other churches or from its context, local and global society. The pre-eminent source of patterned holiness for

the Church is the Eucharist. Particular worshippers in particular local churches at particular moments within the life of the world and the triune life of God, are caught up in complex inter-relation. Their purpose in being church is enabled, despite their own failings and imperfection, through the active presence of God's holiness. In the eucharist is enacted and learned the 'refining fire' of Christ in all these particular circumstances, for the reconstituting of the life of the world in 'multifold inter-actions' (Hardy, 2001, p. 21).

Senge's programme for organizations acts as an invitation to the Church to take an effective part in thinking about and experiment-ing with power relations that show people their true worth. This is achieved through local churches assisting neighbourhoods to build up relationships of trust that counteract fear of strangers or different others. In turn the moral quality of the locality moves from adver-sarial suspicion towards relations of mutual trust, even a readiness to see beyond local need to connect with the wider dimensions of the world. While business is often regarded as essentially selfish (focused on profit), it is clear that much wider considerations, concerning workers becoming more effective as people in cooperation, are increasingly debated and practised.

Blown to bits: depth, range and affinity

In parallel with the learning organization, as an example of chang-ing management practice, Philip Evans and Thomas S. Wurster in their book *Blown to Bits* (2000) offer another illustration that sheds light on the capability of churches and voluntary organizations to re-find themselves in new situations. Evans and Wurster propose that buying and selling of the product known as 'information' lies at the heart of modern business. They argue that, to the extent that information is embedded in physical modes of delivery, a basic law governs its economics; there is a universal trade-off between richness and reach. They define richness as the complex quality of information, as defined by the user, such as accuracy, currency, customization (TV advertising being less customized but with greater reach than the personal sales pitch), interactivity (dialogue in small groups but monologue to a large one), relevance, or security (sensitive information behind closed doors and less sensitive to a wider audience). The precise meaning of 'richness' varies with context but it is clear what it means in each situation.

Secondly, reach simply means the number of people who participate in the particular sharing or exchange of information. They demonstrate how it has been possible to share extremely rich information with only a small group of people and less rich information with larger numbers, but it has been impossible to share *simultaneously* as much richness and reach as one would like. To communicate rich information has required close proximity (usually in the same location) or dedicated channels (proprietary computer networks, retail stores or a sales force), which has obviously limited the number of people with access to information.

Conversely, communicating to a large audience has required compromises in the quality of information. Until recently, technologies have not permitted the achievement, simultaneously, of as much 'richness and reach' as we would have preferred. They offer the example of newspapers reaching a large range of possible customers with limited, static content. Direct mail and telemarketing are considerably richer in customization and interactivity, but much more expensive, and therefore have to be carefully targeted towards those who can afford them. Examples are legion of the manufacturer's trade-off between selling a relatively small amount of high value product to a select few or a lower level of richness, piled high and sold cheap to many people. Evans and Wurster claim that, within a corporation, traditional concepts of control and hierarchical reporting are based on the expectation that communication cannot simultaneously be rich and broad in its reach. Jobs are structured to channel rich communication among a small number of people, organized in hierarchical relationship to one another, and broader communication happens through the indirect routes of the organizational pyramid.

In a burst of technological achievement in both connectivity and standards together, the previous trade-off between richness and reach has been displaced. It is now possible for infinite amounts of high quality information products to be available to customers. Amazon.com, for example, tailors web pages to the known preferences of each customer. As the trade-off between richness and reach explodes previous economic relationships, the organization changes radically. A huge sales force, a system of branches, a printing press, a chain of outlets, or a delivery fleet – which took years and heavy investment to build – suddenly become expensive liabilities. When everyone can exchange rich information without constraints on reach, the channel choices for marketers, the inefficiencies of consumer search, the hierarchical structure of supply chains, the organizational pyramid, the asymmetries of information, and the boundaries of the corporation itself are all thrown into question. The competitive advantages that depended on them will be challenged and business structures that had been shaped by them will fall apart.

This process of transformation has been labelled 'deconstruction'. Evans and Wurster predict that over the next five to ten years, many relationships throughout the business world will deconstruct, as is already beginning to happen. The dismantling and reformulation of traditional business structures results from two forces: the separation of the economics of information from the economics of things; and the disintegration (within the economics of information) of the trade-off between richness and reach. The new economics of information destroys the trade-off between richness and reach, thus blowing the traditional components of business structures to bits. The pieces then recombine into new structures, based on the separate economics of information and things. The authors offer examples in newspapers, retail banking and car sales.

From the perspective of mainline churches there seems to be a close parallel with their capability to provide a rich product over many communities in wide areas. There persists a deeply ingrained expectation, especially in the countryside, that a stipendiary priest, a 'proper' vicar, will be visible and available as the public representative of the Church in religious, school, neighbourhood and pastoral matters. This contradicts many other factors we have referred to already, especially a theology of collaborative ministry against a background of falling clergy numbers. This expectation is hardly surprising since, certainly in the past century, the Church's strategy has been to invest heavily in stipendiary clergy as parish priests in as many places as possible. The richness and reach of the Church has been provided through training, ordaining and deploying as many clerics as possible to be the networked professional providers of religious depth, value or richness. The hierarchically controlled dispersion of clergy has represented the reach or range of the Church's 'information', reinforcing the popular view of clergy as the solo carriers of Christian truth and values, engaged to maintain the Church in its truth and dispense its services to passive recipients.

If this inherited pattern or set of archetypes is no longer to be available, is the Church to be without the capability to fulfil its task? There is certainly a real danger of this when people and priest continue with the despondent notion that somehow they must soldier on with fewer rich resources to cover an ever greater range of territory. The quantity of 'information' available diminishes to match the reducing number of agents of richness. Suppose however that the new environment is in fact a trigger for blowing to bits the old trade-off of inherited patterns. Suppose that richness and reach might be reconfigured. What if all the participants in the Church's worship and life might be considered to be live 'information' or communicators of the gospel spread out in infinite situations? Suppose that local leaders, lay and ordained, whether stipendiary or not, might be re-evaluated as key resources for stimulating and supporting the whole. Imagine that hierarchical triangles of command-and-control no longer reveal the deepest meaning that the Church discovers and enacts in the triune God. Then the Church would find a renewed capability in offering infinite depth, spirituality and meaning across a limitless range of people and places. The *ancien régime* might be blown to bits but the implications of this deconstruction for the Church, in the language of Evans and Wurster, would be 'competitive advantage'.

To sum up so far, through reflection on practice and theories drawn from organizational development and theology, we have outlined some features of a portrait of power.

1   We have described the dangerous adventure of daring to recognize, reflect on and grow in personal and organizational power.
2   An essential role in this, for the Church, is to acknowledge how, recognized or not, patterns of power in personal, family, church, societal and ecological relations have been formed in dialogue with notions of God and God's work in the world. The work of identifying and reforming language and concepts of the divine life, even in a society that claims to be aloof from God, and even when the Church claims to be so powerless, is nevertheless a core vocation.
3   To act truthfully, enacting the meaning to be found in the ways of the trinitarian God with the world, requires attitudes and practices of mutuality, trust and community.
4   Moving beyond maps of power drawn around hierarchy and

domination, we challenge ourselves and society to opt for ways of love and justice founded on that mutual or right relation that is an echo of the trinitarian God and a sign of God's passion for the fulfilment of all creation.

5 Repeatedly we have steered away from the false dichotomy of either trying to find meaning in the reductionism of a simplistic linear explanation or of abandoning all hope of any notion of power other than that of chaos. We have advocated a chaoplexity, or ordered freedom, as a truer reflection of the meaning to be found in God's eschatological purposes for creation.

6 We understand worship, and in particular the eucharist, to be the place where the Christian community is met by God, to be formed over time in its task to free people and organizations to be capable of all that may be required of them.

7 We have recognized the contribution of pioneers both in business, philosophy, education, politics and scientific thought, and in theological and religious theory and practice – through their failures as much as in their achievements – to reconstruct and discover new patterns of energy for organizations and churches.

8 Essentially we conclude that, respecting the different contributions of many and being honest about our failings and desire to dominate, churches, neighbourhoods and society have the capability of repairing the world as part of our fullest life with God whose trinitarian life is the source and sustenance of all living.

So now we must move into a more practical vein of thinking, first about the real capacity of humanity to aspire to work honestly with such notions of power and then to ask what are the characteristics of leadership that emanate from this.

4 | **Capacity**

Worn out

> We have largely lost the sense that our capacity to live well in
> a place might depend upon our ability to relate to our neigh-
> bours (especially our neighbours with a different life-style) on
> the basis of shared habits of behaviour . . . In fact, no real
> public life is possible except among people who are engaged in
> the project of inhabiting a place. (D. Kemmis, quoted in Inge,
> 2003, p. 131)

Earlier we had to face the paradox of a Church never abandoned by
God and indeed sustained by the Holy Spirit in the possibility of
being true to its character and task, and yet clearly constrained in its
purpose through human short-sightedness, lack of courage and
sometimes plain wickedness. Orthodox trinitarian speech identifies
God as Father, Son and Holy Spirit, interweaving energetically with
all life and sustaining all human endeavour that builds up social
life and the flourishing of creation. At the close of Chapter 3 we
showed how the examples of the learning organization and the
deconstruction of former commercial certainties could be recognized
as life-giving forms of renewal, enhancing the capability of both
individuals and organizations. We also have to face the contemporary phenomena of deep suspicion, if not pessimism and anxiety,
surrounding many traditional organizational and institutional
networks and ask if there is a way of holding all the information
together.

Traditional organizations, faced with trans-national competition,
rapid change, a plethora of new legislation, and consumer demands
of many kinds, more than ever have to deal with complex tensions
between the shortage of money, staff, and time to meet increasing
and conflicting internal demand. This is set in a context of a culture,

fuelled by the media, of increasing blame and the myth of infinite compensation. In place of mutual and complex debate, polarities and mutual fear intensify. The general mood that pervades many public bodies, is one of exhaustion, separation and dissatisfaction. In a neo-liberal competitive market, more money for health means either less for defence, or increased taxation or borrowing. Tight budget constraints imposed by central government force local councils to make cuts in services even in the face of apparently increased demand. Increasing numbers of people feel dissatisfied with this model of economy and society; yet, as we have observed in reflection on Maslow's hierarchy, the requirement for immediate satisfaction of the perceived needs of the majority takes priority over loftier or more strenuous debate about the coherence or moral integrity of the structures of power. Churches are inextricably bound into the benefits of the economic system and usually leave it to prophetic individuals or movements to challenge the foundations of the dominant assumptions.

The mixture of idealism and the failure of corporate life was succinctly identified in a 1996 report of research, *Pathfinding Collaborative Inquiry*. A new lifestyle emerged that was characterized by a growing commitment to people-centred, ecologically sustainable development. This is evidenced through new technologies, enterprises, and business management practices. The report strongly opposed inherited methods and attitudes inherent in evaluating economic decisions and progress as fundamentally flawed in their tendencies toward the destruction of the natural environment and local communities, the transfer of wealth into the hands of a privileged minority and the further marginalization and incapacitation of impoverished communities, cultures and spiritual traditions.

Conventional impersonal, linear, and individualist-selfish and exclusivist systems must make way for circular and interlocking models providing a more humane environment for all (Robertson, 1998, pp. 9, 27). An uneasy belief is spreading that unless corporate life is urgently transformed, it will continue to die.

It is not uncommon to hear lament over the loss of the 'better times' of the past and complaint about present difficulty, fearful of the future. However, experience shows that while, inevitably, organizations do die (however hard we may find it to accept this), there is nevertheless a constant stream of new birth and, more critically, a perpetual cycle of renewal and rebirth within existing institutions and world-views. Notably, in the UK, the Beveridge Report led to renewed health-care systems, and similarly there are continual reorganizations of local government, businesses on every scale perpetually restructure to meet new challenges, and organizations of all kinds reinvent themselves in the face of changing circumstances. Yet a mood of pessimism remains in many places, as those within organizations and affected by them suffer under the conflicting tensions created by the ever-increasing pace of change.

In one sense Christian theology is bound to present a vital challenge to this lethargic denial of corporate power and fear of the collapse of goodness and hope in the world. It is the trinitarian God who initiates and maintains the dynamics of relational activity in the world and society and, when allowed to fill and inscribe the ways we live, can reconstitute our vitality. To yearn for the coming of God's reign is to be rightly ambitious for God's purpose to be done in and through all people and places. An unrelenting biblical injunction knows that to pursue individual wealth at the expense of human contact is to create a faceless society where those who are different or unhelpful to our ambition are ignored or swept aside. In worship we contemplate and praise Yahweh for this operational order, without which ordinary life would be impossible (Brueggemann, 1997, p. 336). The spread of new estates of prestigious flats and houses, enclosed and guarded, is one symbol of this closing down between people which is in direct contrast with the enactment of social life when referred to the trinitarian God. Another is the shunning of asylum seekers to the UK, seen simply as human freight (Bradstock and Trotman, 2003). Many categories of people are put on one side, without dignity or worth, regarded as liable only to pull us down.

However, although motivation and energy are God's gift and challenge, theology also has a view about frenetic success at any cost and especially at the expense of the marginalized. Jean Vanier has shown that genuine success includes mutuality, friendship, and care for the marginalized and the different. There must be a particular concern to explore how the Church, as a working out of the Good News and an echo of trinitarian patterning, faces the attrition of its institutions and the terror of irrelevance or extinction. Undoubtedly the traditional churches feel tired – locally and nationally – through the hard work of maintaining models of ecclesiology that daily seem to lose their power. However, as we shall explore later in this chapter, the vocation to live with ambivalence is vital and tough and is achievable only through a conscious interweaving of our life contingently with the temporal world constituted in love by the life of the Trinity. It is a calling to be fathomed deeply in truer understandings of Holy Saturday when the crucified one stands with us in all our limitations and emptiness, helping us to bear God's absence, even though our post-Easter faith tells us that, despite appearances, all will indeed be well. God's own transfiguring life is the ground-base or terra firma of the liminal encounter from which we are urged not to withdraw.

Churches of different denominations constantly generate reports and conferences about the future. Generally, a picture emerges of mainline churches struggling to maintain outworn patterns, attempting the transition to alternative patterns with diminishing resources. Despite upbeat leadership and entrepreneurial work in many local churches, the result is an imperceptible but real reduction in the capacity of the Church even to sustain its own. Discouragement and anger are almost inevitable, when, despite renewed effort, attendance statistics relentlessly decline.

Such experience is not unique. Examining the history of many of our traditional industries, coal, steel or even railways or car-making reveal many of the same tensions and fears currently being experienced by the Church (see, for example, Edwardes, 1983).

The constant activity of maintaining routine worship and pastoral work, balancing the books, and keeping in repair a huge number of ancient monuments is clearly exhausting both clergy and lay leaders, physically and spiritually. An accurate assessment of the level of clergy depression and burnout is hidden, but among leaders in the main churches, serious concerns exist that current demands on the ordained are overwhelming and, in the long term, completely unsustainable (Jackson, 2002). While resources are at full stretch there is little energy, enthusiasm or capacity to absorb more work or even to hear hard facts.

Analysts and internal reviews demonstrate the complexity of the factors affecting the Church's experience. These include, in no particular order of importance, falling stock-markets coupled with rising pension costs, ageing congregations less inclined to leave large residues to the Church than to relatives, fewer people (particularly under 40) offering themselves for ordination, a society that finds no deep meaning in traditional church practice, and a lack of affinity between church leadership and the people who worship. Even exist-ing congregations seem not to be receiving – or are unwilling to receive – the nurture, stimulation and education that could increase their capacity in Christian faith, personally and corporately. The list of issues also includes new legislation of many kinds, such as that enhancing access for the disabled and employment legislation and its bearing on the churches.

Change or die

A key issue for the Church's future is the potential disjunction between deeply ingrained public expectations and renewed patterns of church practice. Two assumptions are to be avoided: that the Church exists severed from its history with people, travelling through time, buffeted but innocent and unencumbered; and, conversely, that everything from the past must be honoured and chaotically carried forward. The complex truth is that the Church must exist for and with its ever-changing context, in plurality and particularity. In every time and place the Church's identity emerges from rediscovering itself in its serving of God's mission.

While society has, in many ways, moved on (some would say back) from earlier notions of ethics, economics, community, spiritu-ality and indeed power, its experience mirrors and throws into relief the unique characteristic and gift of the Church, its Pentecostal abundance, hope, freedom and carelessness about death. In every new situation for the local church there is always a gravitational pull towards the earliest Spirit-led, apostolic communities in the process of discovering how to respond to the deepest meanings to be found in the trinitarian God. Churches are not chameleons, desperately redesigning themselves for survival against attack, but communities of character, endlessly generative as deliberately and courageously they practise the meaning they find in God's life in the world. Mediating holiness in the world is possible only through time given to praise, thanksgiving, silence and worship. Here we are called, held within and transformed so that the dynamic relationality of the trinitarian God can become communion, communication and community (*koinonia*) for re-energizing the world.

The Jesuit Anthony de Mello, for example, offers a striking pattern of prayer and awareness designed to free Christians from attachments and conformity with common judgements of society and of the human heart, replacing them with a freedom formed by God's truth (de Mello, 1998). For a society that largely ignores God, fear and uncertainty in a sense drives an ever faster cycle of positive internal organizational change, in an effort either to prevent the inevitable external change or to give some measure of protection against it. For the Christian, however, there is joy and comfort if we see that the Church is a vital but impermanent companion in God's mission. It exists only as temporary necessary scaffolding for building the Kingdom of God in particular places and times, according to the accounts in Jesus' parables, miracles and personal testimony. Challenging the dominant myths is therefore a significant way to describe its task. In so doing, it is vital to engage with the self-starting energy of God, as witnessed in the Resurrection and Pentecost, to ensure that its legacy in each situation furthers God's coming reign. In the cause of working for *shalom*, robust, prayerful debate, led and contained in safety is absolutely vital. Anxious churches that refuse to 'share the peace' are very perceptive in recognizing the utter commitment and perturbance this would entail.

The malaise in mainstream churches can be recognized, especially by those who work in industry, as part of the general difficulty for organizations experienced over the past 30 years. Businesses under strain have three broad responses to the difficulties being faced: change, amalgamate or die. Nothing remains the same for ever and, from a distance, there appears a constant maelstrom of change, amalgamation, reinvention, death and rebirth. One of the determinants for this is the urgent need to find the capacity to know and meet organizational objectives while allowing for the self-actualization of everyone concerned (Huczynski and Buchanan, 2001, pp. 236ff). Organizations that learn and develop inevitably change through responding to their context while holding to their core purpose. For some organizations change occurs by merging separate operational activities to transform their performance voluntarily, pooling the interests of two sets of owners into one (Lynch, 2003, p. 529). Businesses and voluntary organizations merge for very similar reasons: to expand market share or service provision, reduce overheads, gain economies of scale in production or fund-raising, or absorb wider technologies. One of the main drivers is the need to give organizations the capacity to deliver by turning potential capability into effective action. However, organizations that reinvent themselves solely to survive, in the process may lose sight of their wider mission and objectives. Finding a new direction entails recognizing and drawing out the capability of individuals and groups in the search for the capacity to deliver organizational objectives. Effective organizations increase productivity by developing capability (for example through clearly defined goals and structures, flexible forward planning, meaningful, varied work with learning opportunity or openness) and capacity, combining them in new ways to create opportunities for purposeful action.

This is a constant challenge for secular organizations faced with unwanted, unviable or unsuitable premises and a potentially ever widening gap between the skills of those in the organization and the requirements needed by new technology in the world. These two challenges have been seen particularly clearly in the IT industry since the millennium. In 2000, driven partly by concerns about potential catastrophe in the IT world caused by the millennium itself, the industry boomed. However, within two years most major companies were laying off people, closing premises, retraining and reorganizing in the continual effort to do more with less. So how does the Church respond to the idea of increasing capacity, of doing more with less? The God of impossibilities equips people for their task, remaining faithful even when natural human hope evaporates (Brueggemann, 1997, pp. 413ff).

The recognition that something must die for life to be regenerated is essential. Although not framed in these terms, the world recognizes this essential reality as readily as the Church, a fact reflected in the multitude of literature on strategy and change management. A 2003 review of church buildings in the Chelmsford Diocese reveals huge over-provision with only 1.5 per cent of the population present in an Anglican church on Sunday, occupying only 14 per cent of the seating. Being sure of the facts is tough learning. Urgent questions include: what are we here for, how do we best fulfil our purpose and what buildings, if any, do we need to fulfil that purpose? One way to re-engage churches with the local communities is through (ecumenical) reordering for wider usage. In east London, and elsewhere, the adaptation of churches and attached properties has demonstrated how imaginative leadership, sympathetic architects, benefactors, and local energy can lead to new resources for those communities. Typically, flats for the elderly now complement adequate worship space, together with a doctor's surgery, a playschool, space for neighbourhood committees, and many other possibilities (http://www.chelmsford.anglican.org).

Our aim is to encourage people in the Church and beyond to recognize that change is part of the routine of living. However, for many, the ultimatum 'change or die' seems like a denial that they have genuinely been intending to respond to God's call in their church practice. The assumption may be that if numbers are in decline, the leadership ineffective or the roof insecure, God has abandoned us. Yet the challenge to Christians in any age is to recognize that the coming reign of God is not to be equated with our preferred or inherited pattern of church life. God is as much in the dying to particular forms of church as in regeneration.

Letting go of the panic attempt to sustain particular forms at all costs is being prepared to lose our lives for the sake of the gospel. We have already addressed how often 'church' is mistaken for a particular, historically conditioned social form. If God's plan is demanding and transforming, God will become for us all that is truly necessary for the Church to be a sign of God's purpose. However, we are not called merely to be receptive, waiting helplessly for God to act. Paradoxically, in a world of increasing homogeneity, the shape and colour of a renewed Church will be far less homogeneous than formerly, shaped by local and community needs. Many successful secular organizations, as we have already suggested, increasingly use technology to share the accumulated knowledge of the organization and to mobilize its resources, thus improving overall central oversight while allowing a high degree of sensitivity to local needs.

A growing body of literature speaks of bold visions for more fluid, often much smaller, local expressions of church. We can see the need for mainstream churches to work patiently and mutually (avoiding the dangers of both centrism and localism) towards sustainable new patterns of church and ministry for mission. Evidence suggests that such smaller churches, encouraged and supported by a wider movement, may be more able to reveal God's patterns of interrelatedness through encouraging greater participation, intimacy and expectation in forms of corporate worship, study and outreach. Telling the gospel story through the particular ways of recognizing gifts and distributing tasks could reveal more clearly the liberating potential of church for those who have in recent years chosen to distance themselves from bleak, uninviting institutional forms of 'mainline' Christianity. Across the Anglican Communion differing forms of local, total, mutual ministry, with all kinds of teams and education, have been advance signs of churches that expect more of, and offer more to people. The perpetual danger is that this exploration will collapse into blueprints, fixed forms, and new kinds of clericalism, essentially becoming the new establishment. Increasing bureaucracy is one warning sign of an organization in difficulty; the challenge to bishops and other leaders is not to desire easy answers that bypass the organic task of engaging everyone together in processes of discovery, a mixture of failure and success, sustained in journeys of mutual regard. A deep concern is that mere pragmatism may take the place of corporate attempts to do the kind of theology that invites and excites rather than impedes a wide participation (see, for example, Galloway, 1999; Halloran, 1996; McGrath, 2001; Lobinger, [1998] 2002; O'Brien, 1994; Ward, 2002).

There is a well-known saying in industry that 'a manager's job is to put themselves out of a job'. In other words, they are so to organize things that their role becomes largely unnecessary. (For a short but challenging perspective on this see Blanchard and Johnson, 2004.) For most managers, however, this is anathema as work seems to expand to fit the time available. A particularly difficult piece of dying lies in the hearts and minds of those of us who are paid clergy. However benign, lingering paternalism can lead to subtle abuse of our power to insist on our preferred changes, as we give up too soon on engaging with local insight and wisdom. Dying to pride in our denomination or preferred myth of Christian origins also requires attention. One of the greatest prejudices currently to be overcome is the refusal to recognize as sisters and brothers of equal faith and significance those of denominations other than our own. The Cytun Ministry for Mission Forum in Wales is developing a programme, Companions for a Change, to encourage ongoing discussion about how development plans in each separate denomination might include workable ecumenical projects, especially in rural areas. The question of how churches locally can be persuaded to share ministry across denominational divides is again being faced, despite inherited prejudices. The aims of this bilingual process are to encourage clergy and congregations to move away from a mythologized history of ministry that gives divine preference to their own tradition; to achieve a change in denominational mindsets with regard to shared ministry, e.g. the staffing of vacant pastorates, the primacy of mission over denominational loyalty and survival; to encourage church leadership to motivate congregations along these lines; to open up structured conversation of the issues through study groups; to initiate a process leading to a major national consultation for leaders from each committed denomination across Wales and at every point of authority.

While the Western world might consider it to be healthy competition, for too long churches have disdained one another, often based on an unsustainable historical idealism. Recent scholarship, re-examining the literature of the early Church, reveals a diversity of practice that discounts the homogenizing tendencies of previous generations (Patzia, 2001). There are many strands to ecclesiastical imperialism – social, economic, cultural, demographical and, deepest of all, abhorrence of difference and the desire to be in the 'right' company.

The Lund principle of doing what is possible together gently avoids the tired despair of ecumenism rooted in conflict or the pedantry of detailed written agreements. Instead of denying the validity of each other's orders and eucharist, we could allow ourselves gracefully to grow in understanding and friendship through receiving one another's hospitality without judging. For now we do what is possible, rather than doing nothing because some things seem impossible. God helps us to move beyond calcified prejudice through engaging in prayerful thought (theology) together. One of the current fruits of ecumenical scholarship is that a notion of church rooted in the *perichoretic* communion of the trinitarian God of love is bound to be relational, including not excluding radical difference. Just as no ministry exists apart from its relational character within the catholic Church, no local church exists except within the communion of the Church, historically (apostolic) and geographically (catholic) working for the kaleidoscopic, eschatological unity of all creation. The invitation is for churches, with their particular histories, to be prepared to die for the sake of a single authentic expression of the apostolic Church, genuinely open in diversity to all who are 'in Christ' and free from confessional separation and adversarial debates about 'validity' of orders (Zizioulas, 1985, p. 246). What a difference such dying might make to the Church's witness in every city, town and village across the country.

Practising Christian faith – being gathered and dispersed

Through the Spirit, Christ gives all that is required for human flourishing, in the rich resource of Christian faith. Sharing in God's mission is to companion all people in discovering how to respond to God's invitation to find peace, justice and life in its fullness for all in the widest context of the universe. Christian community is the practice of ordered freedom pouring out of the blessing of God, experienced most intensely in eucharistic celebration, contextually interwoven in all life. Gratitude may be the strand most often absent from contemporary public living. To give thanks is to receive our capacity for living in deliberate resonance with the God who confers the freedom to act truthfully.

The building of such capacity, though a human cooperative venture with and immersion in God's activity, does not usually take the form of an overnight, miraculous transformation – though we should never discount that possibility. Mostly we have to give attention to myriad interactive factors which shape us and those around us, and locate us in particular times and places.

In attending to the reformation of the Church's life we both accept the constraints and insights of the society in which we are contextually interwoven, and expect that the insights we gain from the deep meanings of God's triune life will have a wider influence for the building up of the common life of the world. In that light we re-examine some of the Church's traditional assets to discover how they might provide us with greater capacity than we are currently experiencing. The history of secular organizations, and not exclusively of profit-making enterprises, demonstrates a tendency to treat their resources with a greater degree of rigour and objectivity than does the Church. The Church's resources include

- ordained ministry
- worship and prayer
- scripture and theology
- buildings.

The controversial history of the Church is largely written from the ways in which these have either been mistaken for the main event or have become a millstone instead of a resource. For successful organizations, resources are to be mobilized or discarded in the achievement of clear and unambiguous objectives. Even the most tightly run organization may still find emotional or political difficulty in making optimal use of all resources or of shedding redundant assets and so it is of little surprise that the Church has difficulty in doing so. However, one fundamental role of leadership is alignment of assets and resources with key objectives, so as to ensure that they are effectively used. Yet our key resource is Christian faith itself. The dramatic act of practising eucharistic community, as a conscious Christian contribution towards interpreting and redeeming the world's competitive and adversarial power structures, holds amazing potential for society.

A conceptual legacy of Western individualism is that church is the almost accidental coming together of individuals who 'go to church', as an optional extra to a personal faith in Jesus Christ. This idea is linked with neglect of the essential interpersonal dynamic, within Christian faith, between normal discipleship spread out in everyday living, receiving regular sustenance through frequent gathering for worship, mutual love, care and learning. There follows neglect of the belief that the entire created world is sacred and every moment actively engaged with God's dynamic presence (Sölle, 1991, pp. 42ff). This view has not receded in popular perception, either within or beyond church circles. A continuing and prevailing assumption locates church and especially the ordained, if not in the ecclesiastical building, at least largely in the internal framework of worship, bureaucracy and meetings, with occasional attendance at civic events, raising questions of what it means to be 'local'. As banks, post offices, pubs and garages close in small towns and villages, the church is very often the sole remaining visible sign of a 'local' organization, present for and useful for maintaining the health and meaning of local community.

Increasingly an artificial divide separates Christians 'at church' and Christians in the 'real' world. This further leads to urgent attempts by Christians to read the supposed alien culture of a 'secular society' in an attempt to restore the Church's fortunes, both through better communication and by being less 'churchy'. Paternalistic and paternalizing, as opposed to truly dialogical approaches to mission, mean 'learning just enough about local culture to translate the gospel into local dialects, so you can then teach the natives the one true language of the Church' (Percy, 2003, p. 83).

A consequent problem with this separation of church members in the world from the Church's interior life is the failure to recognize what triggers and sustains disciples. It is a very impoverished diet to be urged to practise discipleship without the nurture of sacrament, scripture, spiritual guidance or direction, and relationship with other Christians. These are the vital experiences and disciplines by which the Holy Spirit brings Christians to maturity, discernment and a commitment and ability to respond to God's call in the world. Immense loss results when churches grimly send people out to 'love and serve the Lord' without all the benefits of regularly being gathered for eucharist. 'The Christian body has no meaning apart from its participation in the body of Christ' (Dale Martin in Hauerwas and Spinks, 1998, p. 81).

The authority of local churches is largely lost when the Christian faith is unexplored by the majority of worshippers. The recovery of God-shaped living and relating lies largely with lay Christians who understand how God is already related to and active in the world. Christian education, locally and contextually rooted as a corporate activity, can help to dislodge the notion of a God who is disengaged or merely visits occasionally. Our real concern is best described as 'affinity' or 'contact'. Human institutions make little headway when they are not properly in touch even with those who are committed to their aims. Commercial enterprises make strenuous efforts, not only through training but by mentoring, goal-setting, appraisal and regular, formal interactive discussion with employees, to ensure maximum opportunity is given for effective participation and inclusion in the organization. It is a real concern to consider that even those who regularly attend church may not be receiving the spiritual nourishment, let alone education or support, they could reasonably expect. Perhaps a dominant cultural or financial group is taking centre stage, unaware of others who feel excluded or less significant, or who have simply disappeared. How can we take responsibility for church communities being widely inclusive and making the effort to notice each other?

Jean Vanier advocates the personal and community benefits of opening ourselves to outsiders or those we perceive to be different. He suggests that, as instinctively as breathing, and usually unconsciously, we avoid those whom we judge to be helpless, inadequate or without worth, precisely because they remind us of our own internal anguish. To bring this process into awareness would be a vital first step (Vanier, 1999, pp. 106–7).

For many years Hugh worked in the transport and logistics industry, with its fast-paced and assertive management style. In this
environment for nearly 20 years he found it impossible to witness,
and indeed the constant pressure to conform in ways unacceptable
to many Christians eventually resulted in his drifting away from the
Church into what he describes as his 'wilderness years'. For him
then the Church seemed to have little relevance as it failed to equip
or support him in the day-to-day context. His hard-working, hard-
playing colleagues formed a strong and mutually supportive team,
and it was inconceivable that he would not participate. It is one
thing for Christian leaders to pronounce against heavy drinking or
other excesses by Christian people but unless the Church equips
them to deal with reality outside the church community, the
Church will always lack relevance. Eventually, being drawn back
into the body of the Church, Hugh has developed a particular
concern about this dislocation between church membership and
the potential witness offered by secular roles. He believes that one
of the greatest challenges for the Church is for it to learn how to re-
engage its members in such a way that their actions in the world,
as the dispersed Christian community, are supported and under-
pinned by tough, critical concern, close community, and prayerful
love. Through such affirmative action the Church may be seen to
know and enact its purpose with vigour.

While a small number of people may gain their conviction of the
truth of Christian faith by logic and rhetoric, for most it is the active
presence of an attractive, loving, worshipping group that has had
the greatest impact. Giving people a new vision of their place in
society and encouraging them in both personal and corporate
endeavour, reveals the latent capacity of the Church as God's gift to
the world.

Many effective organizations encourage mentoring in an effort to
help individuals, and indeed small groups, to understand more
clearly their own strengths and weaknesses and to discern their
future career path. Two parish experiences illustrate this: the first,
largely inspired by Kenneth Leech's *Soul Friend* (1977), is that of
laying out the possibility for most parishioners to have a spiritual
guide. The difference this makes to discipleship and parish life is

incalculable, when ordinary worshippers (fire officers, school caterers, parents, civil servants, teachers, retailers) can have an hour of someone's attention several times a year. Given the security of a safe, confidential meeting, laity can come to expect growth in their faith and Christian practice. Urgent and innovative experiment is needed in this area. Clergy and laity in local churches, with seriousness and humour, can develop simple and safe ways of developing this ministry for mutual benefit. The outcomes will be as various as there are people: reading scripture again, a new way of praying, connecting work and faith, various forms of the ministry of reconciliation, growing in knowledge of Christian faith, wrestling with relationships, and above all knowing that a growing personal faith in God is possible for each one. The skills of listening to recognize how the Spirit works uniquely with each person, can be enhanced by diocesan training for spiritual guides. We believe that this work should become a very high priority in order to increase the capacity of the Church through each person.

The second experience is confidently and lovingly to take time to companion disciples preparing for the sacraments of baptism and confirmation. The Church's capacity is easily diminished when the desire to be baptized, admitted to communion or confirmed is treated as a formality. The revival by Peter Ball, Wim Saris and others in the 1980s of the 'catechumenate movement' in North America, Britain and South Africa, offered the chance to strengthen parish educational processes. Through what is now called the Emmaus Course or process evangelism, the entire worshipping body can be involved in equipping candidates for the sacraments. The combination of experiences and reflection on worship, prayer, Bible study, discussion of everyday life, led by clergy and laity witnessing together, is so much stronger than mere short, formal episodes of teaching by a single cleric. A welcome by the congregation, the giving of a cross to wear, having a sponsor, being warmly treated as well as taught by members of the congregation, keeping preparation vigils, celebrating together, and so on, all contribute to showing that faith is not about knowledge but about God and people in the world together for a purpose. 'Relationships between people are of far more importance than all the "know how" in the world – they are of vital importance' (Saris, 1980, p. 15).

Equipping parents and congregation members to articulate and share their faith more consciously and to ask questions jointly with candidates about how faith might work in the world can only be fruitful. Calling worshippers to learn to take their proper place in society or to see their work as an interaction with God's truth, and working out the practicalities of this, must be a priority. Karl Rahner linked the tangible phenomenon of church with God's work in the world, describing church as 'sacrament of salvation' (Rahner, 1987, p. 412). Jürgen Moltmann's church embodies the roots of hope in a future beyond history, for the whole of history. The Church's task, through word, act and presence, is to repeatedly represent to the civil community a tangible performance of the righteousness and justice of God's coming kingdom (Moltmann, 2003, pp. 30ff).

Johann Baptist Metz's political theology presents the urgent reminder that for Christians, time is finite, and that amid sadness and chaos, God encourages us to collaborate joyfully with the demands articulated in the life and words of Jesus. Opposing the view of Christianity merely as a comfort to the vulnerable, the Argentinian theologian Enrique Dussel suggests that, in conflict with all power abuse that oppresses and diminishes persons and societies, Christian community models 'being with others', the quality of face to face relation that exemplifies the coming reign of God (Dussel in Walton, 1994, p. 144).

Advocating apostolic practice (Acts 2.42–7) and the rich experience of *koinonia*, Dussel describes a way of doing church as a celebration throughout all relationships and forms of life. The eucharistic act of sharing bread especially carries this understanding of a community of disciples at work actively and expectantly in anticipation of Jesus' 'wild hope of human flourishing' (Ford, 1999, p. 148). Essentially the fruits of eucharistic Christian community are practices and habits formed in serving the world's journey to discover the transformational power of the God who raised Jesus from the dead, having earlier raised Israel from Egypt.

To be counter-cultural in this way is not the same as separating world and faith. As notably demonstrated by Ched Myers, gospel community is continually recalled to practise nothing less than the creative and transformative story of God's life in the world. As companions to society, local churches are to show the world how to live a life that is gradually healed of the need to exercise power in ways that dominate; what it means to 'lose my life' in the search for values beyond and greater than myself; to be open to the possibility that those who would lead should content themselves often with following; that leadership should always include humble service; that over time, our eyes are being opened to new ways of being human that are less interested in status, position, titles, and more concerned about 'the other', especially the needy; that we might truly appreciate the distinctive gifts of women as leaders; that we might be 'silenced', as Peter was, into conversion to the servant nature of following and leading; that suffering has the possibility to purge, humble, and save; that we abandon futile competition with others; that we cease to rely on activism and seek the values of contemplation and dependence on God (Myers, 2000). There would be huge benefits if local churches were to improvise on the methods implied in the preface to Myers' (and others') commentary on Mark. For laity widely to be trusted to read scripture together, and to make connections with culture and the practice of life in the world, is surely not too much to expect.

Another antidote to *laissez faire* ecclesiology is to take seriously the promise of Jesus that, on his departure, his disciples would do 'the same works as him and even greater ones' (John 14.12). Suppose we put aside notions of control, reason, objectivity and careful strategy and dare to expect the God of wonders and 'impossibilities' to continue to act, heal and sustain us now. As we struggle collaboratively and individually to be church, in baptism we have already received God's gifts in Jesus' life, death and resurrection and, through the Spirit, made them our own. Jesus' chief gift to us is the ability to be or do what early Christians came to call 'church', *ekklesia*, an assembly of believers intended as a gifted agent of God's purpose.

This commitment lies at the heart of the Church's desire for a unity that enjoys and welcomes the interdependency of difference, in marked contrast to many other organizations and institutions that require a degree of conformity, education, experience and common approach incompatible with Christian values of inclusion. As an extrovert community the Church exists only to exemplify the words and works of Jesus in every human circumstance. As a community of immensely differing people, the Church is routinely stretched to breaking and the exclusion of any who are 'different' is recognized as destructive, again in contrast to many secular organizations less well equipped to encompass the breadth of difference that typifies true Christian community. This community, energized by the dispersed gifts of God through the Holy Spirit, courageously reaches out to welcome, value, cherish and invite all to know and join in God's plan for creation, and therefore struggles against all attempts to marginalize others. The purpose of time spent together in worship and fellowship is to give powerful resources for the major part of the time spent dispersed in families, the neighbourhood and work, struggling for God's justice in the hurt and despair of human living:

> The synagogue and the church have this demanding, awkward task of claiming much more than can be explained. What we have to say is rooted in textual memory and is driven by present pain. This speech insists that the processes of public power where such speech is nullified are a false reality that cannot endure. (Brueggemann, 2000, p. 44)

Christian theology and church practice have a responsibility to speak daringly of a God of love through creating models of hopeful living in the face of human crisis, violence and grief. Holocaust, ethnic cleansing, genocide, terrorism, and victimization of those with mental and physical disability illustrate violent crime perpetrated against those whom it is criminal to attack. The wealthy and advantaged are also victims of violence as the trigger for such discrimination is abhorrence of difference itself. In proclaiming Good News to people in Western society today, describing God as 'powerful' and 'glorious' can no longer serve if they are linked in popular imagination merely with 'above', or 'over against', rather than God as 'with, beside, compassionate, companion and friend'. All words about God are, of course, analogous pictures, scraps of ideas, making no claim to a realistic description of God. But as human life gives rise to, and is formed by notions and practices of authority, the task of mapping life together remains crucial.

Each generation, inheriting scripture and centuries of tradition, has to aspire to finding and living out the meaning it receives and knows from God, critiquing the present in order to discern what has been misconstrued or ignored. Christian communities exist to know their quiet authority through speaking 'rightly' of God. Jews and Christians share language about God that can rightly orientate communities of faith as well as produce from the matrix of their experience 'discourses of emancipatory transformation, pointing to new ways of living together with each other and the earth' (Johnson, 1998, p. 5). As a counter to the classical metaphysical understanding of God, what is required now is a deep interweaving of the trinitarian God characterized by *koinonia* and *perichoresis* with human experience of pain and injustice. Christian communities need to present their memory of God who awakens people to their own dignity, who is and remains compassionately connected with people in every instance of suffering – the murdered innocents, the suffering child, the starving nation, wherever people face barbarous violence and abuse, or fight for justice. A clear parable of a trinitarian approach to relationality is the memory of the authoritative action of Rosa Parks, who helped trigger the American civil rights movement by courageously occupying a bus seat designated for whites.

Johann Baptist Metz, Jürgen Moltmann, Leonardo Boff, liberation and political theologians, have signalled the impotence of 'Almighty God' in the face of the world now, a solitary, ruling male, a single, absolute subject above, observing and remote. Unlike the observer 'God of Enlightenment', the livingness of God as a dynamic of communion is present in all human pain, participating in all endeavours for human happiness and dignity. The cross and Resurrection reveal the trinitarian God's abundant power as a movement of respectful and just friendship, respectful of differences, committed to peaceful resistance to evil and to new beginnings among human brokenness, stirring up new hope, transforming people, and opening up the deep joy of being connected to each other.

This is the love needed through us in ordinary life: in an ethic that is orientated positively toward the other, in questioning war, in sitting with the dying, in compassion that turns into action with the homeless, and in the self in ordinary relationships, year after year. Those who worship such a God cannot be unmoved by suffering or neutral about injustice. If God is three persons in relation, then no human or ecological issue about how the world lives together can be disconnected from faith. Yet the Church is extremely slow to catch up with its own theology. Thousands of those who were brought up as worshipping Christians, now alienated and dissatisfied with religion, are getting on with demanding lives that do not include such practice. While not necessarily hostile to church, they wait for churches to contribute to a public discourse through daring to know their latent power to act or speak relevantly about God and to show a return for the effort of belonging to a Christian community in the midst of demanding and conflicting human responsibilities and fears. An undemanding agenda has proved a false trail, lacking in any kind of power: not least the power of authority, strong in its own awareness of faith and hope. There are no external, mechanical innovations for ailing churches. Just as secular organizations that lose the focus on their 'core business' wither and eventually disappear, so soothing and understated churches that don't speak directly of God's uncompromising holiness and celebrate the trinity-shaped difference between the world's peoples will eventually die. Contemporary Western culture requires Christian communities to voice and enact God's truth about people in relationships as an alternative imaginative contrast and awakening challenge. At the beginning of the Great Thanksgiving in the eucharist, abandoning all caution we throw down the challenge, 'The Lord is here!' Yet we need to learn again how God can be our root and core focus.

Clergy – a key resource for Church and society

Leaders in all walks of life are critical enablers, recognizing potential capacity and releasing it for action. This key role of leadership is an area that commercial organizations, in particular, have sought to develop at least over the past quarter century. Likewise the major leadership resource into which the Church has traditionally poured so much effort is ordained ministry. Denominations differ in their language and expectations, but there is a sense among all the traditional churches that disproportionate expectations are placed on the clergy, often to the detriment of everyone else. Many experiences of stimulating and accompanying reflection on the role of clergy show how diverse are the ideas, feelings and practices associated with priesthood, the presbyterate or ordained ministry. In debate we often refuse to avoid the false dichotomy of believing that if the role of laity is enhanced, the role of clergy must therefore be diminished. We wish to register two particular issues, concentrating chiefly on the second.

First is the particular role of the clergy in evoking and encouraging the gifts and responsibilities of laity in daily life, and specifically church work. There is a steady stream of radical new literature exploring the current and future possibilities for the practice of priesthood. The more that is expected of the laity, we argue, the more will be expected of the clergy, in new and imaginative approaches to oversight or episcope. New patterns of collaborative ministry between clergy and laity are configured on this basis. However, transition is hard. Overworked, self-believing, omnicompetent leadership can foster a toxic atmosphere of panic and strain, even when linked with the rhetoric of becoming a 'collaborative' church. Still prevalent hierarchical structures and attitudes, no matter how avuncular, can only repeat the authoritarian culture and practices of the past.

As Anglicans, vitally open to all with whom we can have common cause, we are committed to people in localities continuing to find real and practical expression for their cooperation with God's work in the whole of life, personally encountered in Jesus Christ and distributed by the Holy Spirit. We believe that although the future of the Church must continue in localities, the inherited parish system needs to be richly amplified by many imaginative possibilities through house groups, extra-parish assemblies, festivals, schools, colleges, chaplaincies and renewal movements, meeting wherever and whenever appropriate. Experience shows that those known as leaders, and how they lead, make a critical difference in all human endeavours and not least to the authority of the Church, in both its surrounding context and authenticity in proclaiming the gospel. Edgar Schein describes such leaders as *Animators* (Schein in Hesselbein et al., 1996, p. 60). The role and place of leadership, being ever better understood and applied in secular organizations, has already changed in many organizations from the demagogic control of the nineteenth century to a more subtle, often more human-centric style in which the place of all *stakeholders* or the more gentle term, *constituents* is recognized and honoured (for example, see Nanus' article on vision in Kouzes, 2003, pp. 351ff). In some respects the Church lags behind in its thinking on leadership, but the Church's authority to contribute to the debate on power distribution in the world lies generally with the practice of local churches, in radical ecumenical and respectful partnership. Recognizing their vital and developing vocation in society, they require leadership that, through openness to God and to the various human disciplines, from psychology to economic theory, by which people explain the world, can allow itself to be authoritatively reinvented in non-traditional ways. Leaders placed in positions of regional authority urgently need to lead the reshaping and story telling of what church can be for people in particular situations (see Chapter 5). They cannot be effective as 'teachers' or 'artists' if their time is spent managing and maintaining the inherited system.

The second aspect is the iconic role of the clergy for the Church, for the committed worshipper and for society. Clergy in the traditional churches vary, personally and systemically, in how far they understand their primary role as being for the Church itself or for wider society. As we have already noted, reform of the Church and the work of the Church in and for society is highly determined by the theory and practice of ordained ministry. The Church still tends to make changes by identifying areas of dissatisfaction, thinking through new visions and issuing directives to implement decisions. Despite the alienation of many clergy from their vocation, the Church still has little appetite and few resources for examining the psychological dimensions of change. Notable exceptions include the empirical studies of Anglican psychologist-theologian Leslie Francis and of the Jesuit psychiatrist Luigi Rulla. In collaboration with others, Francis has undertaken painstaking observation of the personalities and stresses of clergy and congregations, importantly recording the wide range of reasons why people abandon church membership. Yvonne Warren and Neil Burgess in their work have identified the despair, isolation and low self-esteem that many clergy experience on a daily basis (Warren, 2002; Burgess, 2002).

Rulla's interdisciplinary approach to the formation of priests and religious mediates between two central notions. The first is that all Christian vocation is a decision to cooperate with God (Jeremiah 31.31; Ezekiel 36.26) in each person's life work of self-transcendence in the manner and power of Christ (Galatians 2.20). Rulla differentiates a notion of self-development based on individualistic ambition and one based on self-transcendence as 'ultimate *communion with God'* (Egenolf, 2003, p. 85). The second is that this partnership with Christ for transformation is often limited or impaired. C. G. Jung uncovered, in his study of hidden patterns or archetypes of the collective unconscious, the conflict between the overt values of a priest or institution and the shadow side. Similarly, Rulla has drawn conclusions from researching the inconsistencies between the conscious ideal and unconscious real-ego. One of his most significant conclusions is that clergy can, for their own security, continue to hold to their formal office even when genuine respect for and belief in its meaning has dissipated. Rulla believes that the Church would increase its capacity to act if clergy were given time and resource to work through their psychological blocks. It is better for those locked in an inappropriate vocation to have the chance, through both

psychological and spiritual means, either to internalize the values or to move to another that enables them to find inner freedom and become personally genuine. This places great demands on all concerned with both initial and continuing vocational formation (college staff, spiritual guides, tutors, training incumbents), both in their work with each cleric and in their own responsibility for growing in self-awareness. Generalist staff also need to be able to see therapists, psychiatrists or counsellors without the disparagement this can sometimes generate within the Church. Priestly formation, for too long dominated by pure academic training, is therefore about the entire person in all their relationships with God and other people. Rulla's *Anthropology of the Christian Vocation*, although specifically dealing with the Roman Catholic Church, invites a far wider response from those responsible for the increasing maturity of the Church.

A key question implied by Rulla's findings and relating to structural change, is: how can bishops and dioceses work across this interdisciplinary matrix of psychiatry, theology and spirituality to help unlock clergy from fixed roles in order to be flexible and ready to lead the Church in ever new situations?

Clergy, like all public figures, operate within a persona given them by the Church or community. Offence occurs when office holders sit light to inherited expectations or when the Church makes moves to unravel the archetype. Jung outlines the dangers for those who become so immersed in the role that they lose their capacity to act spontaneously or to recognize their shadow side that does not fit the role. Through studying the archetypes of the collective unconscious, Jung came to believe that, despite every denial, humanity possesses a natural religious function. Clearly Jung is not speaking here of doctrine or confessional belief, but of an attitude of mind about dynamic powers that call for devotion, worship and love (Fordham, 1972, p. 71). Jung saw the function of religion, which it achieved to a greater or lesser extent, as providing satisfying forms to meet the human need for repentance, sacrifice and redemption. In a sense that is easily recognizable in everyday life, he saw the role of religious structures and representative persons as to protect the public from being overwhelmed by the expectation that they should share in the representative task previously assigned to the clergy. How able are laity to face for themselves the full impact of the experience of 'God'; why is there such deep-seated resistance to such moves by church leaders and thinkers? He fears that laity faced with the full force of religious experience, in extreme cases, could be led to insanity (ibid., p. 72).

There are important issues here about awareness. How free are the churches to make fundamental changes in their habits? Do theological concepts and practices of collaborative ministry make impossible demands on laity? However, we limit discussion to the particular pressure for clergy in fulfilling their role for others while being true to themselves. For many in the Church the perception is that spirituality and perhaps even ethics are the domain solely of the Church, and yet many strong leaders hold equally strong ethical and spiritual positions within their non-spiritual organizations. Such leaders, and the organizations in and for which they work, recognize the need to develop individual leaders and to allow them to explore new roles and areas of development (see, for example, Bolman and Deal, 2003a). In contrast traditional theological training, currently being severely critiqued, has tended to prepare candidates for ordination, and assumes that the priest largely inhabits a single role, with almost 'magical' power, expressed in living a strangely separate life, wearing robes, being expected to speak and act in an exemplary manner, to be present at community events, and to be available unless physically absent 'on leave'. This is a caricature but the picture is reinforced by humour that only has an impact when it reveals the truth. So TV comedy clergy work best when they palpably fail to maintain the role (*The Vicar of Dibley* or *Father Ted*) or when they so maintain it that there is no longer any personal residue (the Vicar in *Dad's Army*). Detective stories such as *Inspector Morse* need buildings and clergy who act out the archetypes thoroughly in the face of sin and violent death; yet soap operas have a penchant for clergy who are so 'themselves' that they hardly bear the public archetype. If Jung's theories have any validity, clergy need support to balance the many conflicting demands made upon them by 'God', the bishop, other clergy, worshippers – not to mention friends or family – all with varying degrees of understanding and the desire to be a warm, full human being.

In this study of power relations we have placed an emphasis on the value of learning to be 'real' as a way of transformation for people and organizations. Empirical data shows how frequently clergy fail to maintain the values of their official role and act out their shadow side. We should not think of this as unique to the clergy. Leaders in all enterprises experience many of the same doubts and disorders but other organizations (certainly the larger ones) are often more able to accommodate, support or in a last resort enable a parting of the ways that is, as far as possible, both supported and humane. Disorders of priesthood expressed in sexual problems, depression, fear of authority and obsession with success or failure, often reveal a struggle to be human in intimate relationships. Although some of the problems surrounding priesthood are unique, clergy may not be as exceptional as has often been thought, but ingrained social expectations of the priest as removed from normal human problems are greater. Reflections on priesthood may indeed hold value for those who work in other institutions and organizations.

We have recalled how God's power is shown in weakness (2 Corinthians 12.9–10) and how living honestly with failure can be the surest learning. Dying to old forms of exercising personal and institutional power is a demanding but vital summons. As Jesus was stripped for his crucifixion, and as God is revealed in suffering, those of us who are clergy have a responsibility now to be courageous in standing on the threshold of transition and to face metamorphosis. It is nothing new to claim that challenges are opportunities sent by God. Comfort lies in the fact that God generously gives the capacity for the quality of change in which some of the old inheritance is trustworthy and can be reliably brought forward into the new. South American sourdough bread offers an image in which part of yesterday's dough, kept back and used in today's, provides precisely the yeast required for the germination of a new loaf. Identifying the content of what can be preserved and reworked is what requires discernment.

Poets, musicians, writers, athletes, wood carvers and sculptors know how creativity arises through waiting and living with painful tension. What is lost in terms of peace, certainty, prestige or sleep is replaced by the capacity to live with ambivalence, doubt and endless new opportunities. In Chapter 2, we explored the controversial notion that God creates precisely within chaos rather than from nothing. This comes into its own as we invite clergy and other Christians to put aside nostalgia for the past, recognizing that automatic prestige has little to do with the trinitarian God of vulnerable interconnectedness. Personal stories, liturgies and rituals for coping with liminality, and the new liturgical emphasis on keeping Holy Saturday as opposed to its being just a transition between Good

Friday and Easter Day, all testify to the possibility of treading new paths if God, though hidden, is sharing the struggle. Instead of the former view of clergy as having almost magical prestige in society, they are now often presented as mostly irrelevant and banal and not infrequently as perpetrators and power abusers.

Jung would ask, if today priests are experiencing marginalization, what is it that society as a whole is thereby wanting to repress and reject? Priests require courage to 'encounter the shadow, the dark and negative side of an archetype' and this is extremely important work for the Church to be offering for the growth in health of society as a whole. The American psychotherapist William Perri sheds light on this discussion of capacity. Although writing out of experience of work with celibate clergy and expressing little interest in the priest as animator and evoker of the practical ministries of others, we find his work insightful in studying the transformation of ordained ministry generally. Perri highlights the traditional theological approach to priesthood rooted in three rich aspects: messianic, prophetic, and sacrificial. It is these qualities perhaps, above all others, that differentiate the priest from leaders of other kinds of organizations. This is not to say that other leaders do not or cannot exhibit these qualities in part but here is one of the great offerings that priesthood can in a sense offer to the world in general, and the world of leadership in particular.

First, the messianic task of bearing a message of reconciliation is a vital element in the priestly role, clearly articulated in ordination liturgies as a forgiving or binding as part of the gift of the Holy Spirit (John 20.22–3). Although churches differ in their understanding and practice of the sacrament of reconciliation, mediating God's for-giveness in the community is a vital function. In a culture of blame and litigation, the world needs to know God's infinite forgiveness. The shadow side appears when priests from their own vulnerability boost their own egos, abusing their power in binding others in patterns of authoritarianism. When priests become depressed, one possibility is that they are withholding mercy and forgiveness from themselves. Part of the messianic task, suggests Perri, is to ensure the handing on of the tradition, which is beginning to be rediscovered as a role of the secular leader, although described in terms of passing on something more than the corporate culture (see, for example, Bolman and Deal, 2003a). To be effective in this mediation, priests require to be aware both of their own tendency to control and of the antidote, which is flexible knowledge of the huge variety of Christian thought and practice over the centuries. The messianic calling implies a growing capacity for intimacy with God through prayer, and a deepening connection with self in a spirit of acceptance and with others in all their difference. Finally the priest shows the community the humility of not knowing all the answers or attempting to carry the world alone. An important dimension of this is to show everyone the art of forgiving and forgetting so that all can work for freedom and peace.

Second, a messianic prophet who cannot truly animate others will be constantly irritated and congest the growth of others. Jesus the Messiah calls would-be disciples to deny themselves, using the same Greek words as Luke uses for denial-betrayal (Luke 22.61). The Letter to the Galatians claims that part of the radical calling of prophetic figures is to be insecure to the point of death, with confidence, rather than in a spirit of anxiety, 'It is no longer I that live, but Christ who lives in me' (Galatians 2.19–20). Perri believes that only priests consciously in touch with their own pain will be able to achieve the non-anxious insecurity that can be of service to others. This essential self-aware creative angst is what releases a priest (and therefore all people) to stand apart, not in superiority but to be self-possessed and not falsely meeting the supposed expectations of others:

> The terrible guilt feelings of the depressed person are existential, that is, they represent the failure to live one's own life, to fulfil one's own potential because of the twisting and turning to be 'good' in the eyes of the other. The other calls the tune to one's eligibility for mortality, and so the other takes up one's unlived life. (Perri, 2003, pp. 31–2)

The prophetic figure is not to be tamed by social convention and does not fit with heroic expectations. As Jesus, in the spirit of Isaiah, brought good news to the poor, the priest's task only has meaning in the capacity to bring hope to society. A strong feature of survival in secular organizations is the temptation merely to 'toe the line', to avoid criticism or challenge of corporate and managerial decisions that go against either ethical or corporate considerations. This is changing and the prophetic role, often dressed in terms of business ethics, is becoming a major factor in investment decisions, stock market dealing, environmental concerns and people management, to name but a few. The challenging, positively critical, prophetic role of the priest is one that can be encouraged in lay people as well as ordained and in the workplace as well as the church.

Third, the sacrificial priest has to be both wounded and a healer. Otherwise, the picture of God and the model of ministry portrayed and imitated becomes one of arrogance, unremitting energy and supposed immunity to illness. When a priest comes to believe in this invulnerability, depression and pessimism can soon follow. Giving up on pretending to be totally dependable and Atlas-like is a requirement for priests who want to build up real humanity in others. 'Sacrificial' lives can become anxious manifestations of an inflated ego unless there is a reflective discipline of prayer. An essential element in this is the obligation of priests to understand sacrifice, not by assuming a personal role as victims and martyrs, but authentically by taking ownership of their own pain, thus showing the world how to take personal responsibility for woundedness and grief in the interconnections between people. In the business world such integrity of self-knowledge is widely expected, although again the language differs, such ideas being expressed in terms of enabling or service. We explore this further in Chapter 5. But, as with other areas of the priestly role, modern leadership gurus are still feeling their way to a comprehension of what the Church already understands. What is now required is a description that expresses the priestly role in inclusive language accessible to those beyond church-based clerical roles.

Despite the background of celibate priesthood, Perri's insights into the difficulties encountered by clergy in becoming agents for change have resonances for other churches. Studies among Anglican ordinands reveal that self-aggrandizement and a desire to be perfect are not uncommon. Research into antisocial behaviour among clergy reveals high degrees of concern about personal authority, a tendency to be judgemental and to have low opinions of parishioners. Andrew Greeley and Douglas Hall in separate research show clergy as having real difficulties with authority. Rulla, convinced that episcopally directed change cannot occur unless clergy as human beings are truly free to follow, finds tendencies towards rebelliousness and narcissism among seminarians (Perri, 2003, pp. 56ff).

Human beings who feel victimized and insecure seek to have power over others and to dominate. There is growing evidence and reflection on how this is expressed sexually as a form of power abuse (Ammicht-Quinn, Haker and Junker-Kenny, 2004). Taken cumulatively, research reveals that the misuse of power and authority masked as piety is a marked characteristic of priestly leadership, and that these features are not uncommonly reflected in leaders in other disciplines. This may be one major factor in the loss of credibility of the Church as well as having precisely the potential to build its capacity. Perri proposes that the true work of priests can be regained when, instead of isolation, they can be helped to find intimacy with themselves, others and God. Anglican experience in the UK over several decades resonates with the concerns of Perri about clergy with narcissistic personalities who find it difficult to have connections that are more than superficial. Clergy in hierarchical life tend to be 'passive-receptive, insecure, conforming, and have a high need for nurturance' and to develop habits of passive resistance and immature behaviour with one another and their superiors (Perri, 2003, pp. 74ff). They naturally form patterns of competition and pretence in order to further their ambition to take control over their lives and hopefully be in control of others. The creative role of clergy to mediate God's hope in Church and society depends on them being sufficiently in touch with others, daring to relinquish positions of power over others, in order to really live. Perri's positive argument is that the symbolic archetypal character of clergy is a vocation to stand on the border between life and death, strength and weakness, male and female, adult and child, perfection and hopelessness, responsibility and irresponsibility. Priests have the particular responsibility for helping guide individuals and the whole community beyond the foothills of contact with one another and with God, to deeper or more contactful levels of social and psychological integration. They may be thought of as liminal persons because they are called to live at the threshold between two worlds. They enact this by their public presence at events critical within the life cycle of individuals, churches and societies, especially at points of change in identity when their task is to name and make this clear (e.g. at a baptism, the opening of a new counselling service or the development of a public amenity).

The ordained have the task of leading the Church in moving away from the unconscious one-sidedness that prevents real contact with the heart of people. The upheaval of choosing the integrated way of becoming real and living in creative chaos is a key offering of clergy for the metamorphosis of the Church, choosing its own demise, crucified for the world. To reconnect with society will require the sacrifice of priests dying in order to rediscover themselves, but nothing in the end can be said of public ministries that is not also profoundly true for each worshipper within the whole Church.

Living in the true self

A huge opportunity currently faces the mainline churches deadened by approaching life so cautiously. Fearing to die, we fear to live. Cooperation, collegiality and collaboration are words used frequently by church leaders advocating change, yet all the episcopal and synodical rhetoric in the world can have little power unless each committed church person is invited to embark on a journey on which they face being broken open to discover emptiness, liminality and creative chaos. If the Church performed the sacraments with more bodily confidence so that, for example, baptisms were by total immersion, confirmation took two years of disciplined formation, eucharist involved less timorous quantities of bread and wine, and ordination liturgies revealed more of the chaotic blend of clergy and laity, we might expect more of the livingness of God to disturb and console deeply. Frances Young rightly commends the particular experience of the L'Arche communities as a sacramental sign of the joy which churches are generally denying themselves (Young, 1997).

The challenge to clergy to live with ambivalence is also a vital clue to the Church's understanding and enactment of power for society. Throughout this study we have proposed that the world needs evidence, from the practice of Christian faith in communities, that love, happiness, gratitude, engagement and joy are possible and viable based on the pilgrimage of deconstructing the 'false self'.

Each person, going down into the water, as Christ went down into the Jordan to be given his vocation in the power of the Spirit, becomes part of a community that hears God's Word. The challenge of following Jesus (John 21.18–19), alternately electrifying and terrifying the first disciples, entails the choice to surrender to Christ. Paul bids us cry with Jesus in the Spirit, 'Abba! Father!' as a sign that we choose to be children of God and joint heirs with Christ (Romans 8.14–17). This is the uniqueness of Christianity, not as dogged adherence to some ideal but as an encounter or relationship with the Mystery of God. Paul's choice of the Greek word *baptizestai* insists we are drowned, shipwrecked, soaked to the skin in the death of Christ. The crucifixion was the place where Christ owned his responsibility. To be crucified in him means we actively share responsibility for God's coming reign. This requires in us Christ's own self-denying way of life (Mark 8.36). We are unsurprised to find, in the most compelling current 'secular' work on leadership, an appeal for leaders to develop 'a heart of character'. An integrated sense of self, respect and concern for others, sensitivity to feelings, wearing power lightly, and knowing their deep inner worth are all elements of a root foundation, in most people one that is far from complete, but which lies at the heart of leadership (see Cammock, 2003, pp. 136ff).

Learning to live in the true self is largely the work of prayer. Many kinds of praying take place but the Church's capacity leaks away when the fuller possibilities for encouraging everyone to pray with more discipline and expectation are not pursued. A particular avenue for adult spiritual growth with links to the invitation to find the true self is found in the experiential reflections of William Johnston, M. Basil Pennington and Helen Thompson. The world needs the Church to do what it claims to do: to be centred on God, to know God as friend and to expect deep union as the active power for living (Pennington, 2000, p. 123).

Money and property

The main UK denominations, in contrast to any secular organization (other than those such as the National Trust, set up specifically for the purpose) have a burdensome responsibility for maintaining local churches, burial grounds, vicarages and halls. Whatever the age of church buildings they are subject to dilapidation, demographic change and the varying strength and size of a worshipping congregation, as well as some degree of interest from government and other authorities. Wealthy rural congregations, making provision for tourists and pilgrims, can maintain a listed medieval building while in other circumstances a once fine resource is incapable of attracting grant funding.

The Church in Wales, for example, currently has some 1,490 churches (of which 7–10 per cent are Grade I or II* listed), mostly used for a few hours a week. The Representative Body (as owner of the buildings) will soon be unable to subsidize the costs of the maintenance of ministry as it has previously. The resultant incremental increase in parish contributions is likely to result in many church councils no longer being able to afford the running costs and major repairs of the local church building. Central funds for fabric repair, such as Cadw and the Heritage Lottery Fund, are being reduced, the former questioning the Welsh National Assembly's commitment to the built heritage. Even more significant is the absence of any body responsible for developing a national policy. Architectural historians and conservators often seem determined to look through only one lens in their approach. Some agencies (such as the Victorian Society or the Georgian Group), while making no significant financial input into the maintenance of churches, under legislation are afforded considerable influence over the internal ordering of listed buildings, often preventing greater freedom in the use of a building. When listed churches reach the end of their useful life there is a presumption against demolition which, although understandable in the case of Grade I and II* churches, begs the question of whether a more realistic policy is needed so that the burden of maintenance of moribund buildings does not prevent the maintenance of the rest.

To maintain a building in a time warp is to ignore any sense that history is contingent and contextual and that each generation has, until now, been free to place doors, windows, monuments, altars, pulpits, choir stalls, screens, steps and seating wherever they were required. The intriguing interest in church buildings for many is not as churches but rather how, through many different reshapings, lovingly and often eccentrically achieved, they reveal the development of meanings held at different points by particular local people and communities. So to maintain the Victorian pews, themselves often later and radical alterations to a much earlier building, against the needs of the church to be true to itself now, is to take an absurdly myopic viewpoint. Power over and responsibility for the future of buildings are polarized rather than unified, and unless conservationists consider the burdens they place on small congregations they may well precipitate the closure they most seek to avoid. This is not an issue that can be sorted piecemeal. Locally each church or group of churches must decide its own needs; nationally, there needs to be focused cooperation across the field between government, local planning authorities, amenity societies and the churches. In Wales the National Assembly is uniquely placed to deal with this burning issue, one that affects the whole of society, not simply the churches and not merely for heritage reasons but for the whole life of the nation.

The church is rich in people, buildings and money if it can find a way of reconfiguring how to live out of its true capacity. Again in Wales, the Bishop of St Asaph, addressing the 2004 diocesan conference, looks for realism, thanksgiving for a wealth of talent, and a dependency on God that makes living with risk sustainable and growth a priority (*Teulu Asaph Special Report*, August 2004). For all organizations (as for people), this is always the challenge of the moment triggered by self-criticism or dissatisfaction that goes beyond depression and self-pity. How can we live more fully to meet our potential? How do we move from here to where we want or need to be? In general, organizations operating comfortably don't ask such questions, at least with any great degree of seriousness. However, when complacency is replaced with discontent, either through regular self-review or through significant and imminent external pressure, change becomes a matter of urgency.

Moving forward

For years Marks & Spencer monopolized the UK high street, as the store of quality. Recently it has been forced to accept the reality that its many competitors have also been working to deliver quality products at a competitive price. The result has been that M&S, rather than continuing to lead and with an opportunity to influence events, rapidly found itself under pressure, with little room to manoeuvre. Highly skilled workers, a large number of strategically placed buildings, a large income, well-developed systems, and responsive and loyal suppliers are all signs of capability. M&S found itself in much the same situation as the mainline churches, with well-developed capability but, squeezed by events and context, having insufficient capacity to respond quickly to the crisis.

In a sense, like the Church, the difficulty facing M&S is a short-term lack of capacity. Change is not easy, comfortable or achievable in a timescale not of M&S's choosing. Shareholders, competitors and customers all exert pressure for rapid change in an organization more used to evolution than revolution. The Church faces similar pressures. Competitors, 'other attractions' like Sunday shopping (Elizabeth Rigby, *Financial Times*, 25 August 2004, p. 4) that compete for people's time and energy, constantly reduce the capacity of the Church to respond by drawing alert and sensitive people to new loyalties and agendas. The customer, the 'ordinary' person in the street, increasingly bored at finding nothing desirable in the store, moves on. Like an ailing retailer, the Church remains a large organization with great capability but increasingly constrained in its capacity for action.

Despite the similarities with Marks & Spencer, one great difference remains. M&S has gone to great lengths deliberately to ensure that its leaders have the capability to make urgent and radical executive decisions to reverse decline. This might include selling parts of the business, outsourcing, changing sales and marketing strategies, closing stores, disposing of buildings (or moving to new ones) or making redundancies. To any effective board of directors no part of the business can be exempt from scrutiny or so sacrosanct that major change cannot touch it.

In similar situations, the Church generally acts differently. For example, church leaders frequently disclaim their power to change aspects of the organization; local people often choose not to see the wider picture; tensions and controls within the Church are significantly more subtle than in any commercial organization. Although the leaders of the Church may declare new policies, the cumulative effect may well be an empty church, rebellious clergy or threats to withhold income. In the light of our study on power, we can recognize that individual leaders are unable to effect results by exerting traditional hierarchical levers of power – statements, threats and ultimatums. This situation therefore requires a much more subtle and holistic approach bringing alternative strategies into play, and we consider these in Chapter 5 when we discuss ideas of 'adaptivity'.

However, in one significant dimension of church life today leaders do exercise very direct power over those contractually employed in the crucial tasks of education and development, either in colleges or as diocesan education and training officers. To make aligned paradigm shifts, the churches recognize their need not only of local church leaders in parishes and new projects, but also of those with experience and daring in knowing where to make interventions (intellectual, emotional and practical). However, in current structural changes responding to the 'Hind Report', *Formation for Ministry within a Learning Church*, approved by the Church of England General Synod in 2003, many of these posts are vulnerable. To work in this critical area requires an especially developed self-awareness. In the process development, mission and ministry officers will have made themselves vulnerable in that their role has a particular charismatic quality and is very dependent on the goodwill and understanding of the current bishop.

In the earlier discussion on priestly anxiety, we concluded that an essential Christian calling is to learn to live without security yet without becoming a victim. In business and society generally, the employment status of consultants and educators is insecure. Why should the Church be any different? One of the tasks of the Church is to show the world how to be more ethical in the ways people are treated. The Church and its leaders must face their particular responsibility for the lives of others and their dependents. Ineffective and unsuitable post holders cannot be supported, but the Church owes society a model of the highest standards in responsible employment and people management, as one of the surest signs of its understanding of the triune God. We hold that senior staff need to keep very closely in touch with those who resource the Church through education, research, training and strategic development, critiquing them privately and supporting them publicly while they usefully fulfil this liminal vocation.

The Church is the largest voluntary organization in the UK; it is also a major land and property owner. Certainly not just in terms of physical and financial assets but of people (with deep wells of spirituality, education and experience) the Church in the West remains a significant institution. With these assets at its disposal the Church has no grounds for denying its power. We have noted recurrently that these assets are failing in their potential and that the Church has difficulty connecting with people. Despite the problems of maintaining the present infrastructure and staffing, the capital, property and annual income of the mainline churches would be the envy of any new voluntary or business venture. Imagine for a moment the announcement of such a new venture, having the combined resources of all the churches, for the creative promotion of its espoused purpose. Not only would it make international headlines but organizations and institutions would be suggesting creative partnerships and alliances. One of the greatest challenges in an environment such as the UK is the complexity and interdependence of the institutions of state and the wider social and economic networks. That the Church could begin again is a pure fantasy. However, the God of regeneration and new beginnings can give the Church the capacity to sharpen its purpose and resolve.

5 | **Adaptivity**

The power to change

> In a bewildered world the church has an urgent task of gathering the fragments, listening to what the dominant myths have excluded: the task of soul-making on personal, communal and socio-political levels must be at the heart of the becoming church. (Grey, 1997, p. 15)

An essential part of the Church's evangelism is to re-examine and turn away from all performances of power as domination, looking instead to the fostering of public practices of mutuality in everyday life (Forrester, 2000, p. 113). This chapter explores some current thinking around the 'adaptive organization' in relation to the theological work of earlier chapters. The term 'adaptive' is being used in a particular sense that will emerge, rather than to suggest that the Church can take any form to suit circumstances. In order to succeed, the adaptive organization has leadership requirements that both resonate with and challenge Christian community practice.

Despite a wide disenchantment with heroic leadership, there is a growing recognition of the impact of leaders. Ernest Shackleton, in his leadership of the transantarctic expedition (in which the 300-ton *Endeavour* sank on 21 November 1915), signals many of the recognized disciplines for effective leadership. Rob Mackintosh of the Leadership Institute has summarized and developed for application within the Church, the core disciplines that against great odds resulted in every member of the Shackleton expeditionary team returning home. The leader self-differentiates within the organization, subordinates self to higher principles, exercises self-management, creates trust within the organization, invests in keeping morale high and communication open, shapes an effective team, undertakes continuous renewal, creates the working climate of the organization, seeks out sources of energy and information (Mackintosh, course handout, Cambridge, August 2001). In a world where change has become the only constant, effective leadership is vital as a 'universal process that involves all of us and in which we all have responsibility' (Cammock, 2003, p. xiii). Shackleton, through his own internal struggles and sense of responsibility, ensured that every member of the team used their particular human force rather than merely performing allotted tasks.

Reductionist forms of leadership that relegate individuals to being mere cogs in a wheel model a purely mechanistic notion of work. Even the desire for an efficient factory must resist the objectivizing fantasies of Taylor's 'Scientific Management'. Pragmatically, as 'information' shapes behaviours in an increasingly affluent society, conscious of 'rights' and less tolerant of the 'one size fits all' approach, organizations seek to mobilize latent power through the active participation of all. This adds up to more than employing temporary workers to bypass employment law or putting jobs off-shore as a financial response to cost differentials between countries, in the interests of greater efficiency. Information-based organizations, theoretically, contrast with the older systems that 'used' individual workers without involving them personally. Drucker for example argues that what makes a university great

> is that it attracts and develops outstanding teachers and scholars, making it possible for them to do outstanding teaching and research. The same is true of an opera house . . . a new conductor makes productive what he has inherited, by working with individual orchestra members and groups of instrumentalists . . . it is the conductor's people skills that make the difference. The workers are not labor, they are capital. (Drucker, 2002, p. 76)

Almost every conversation with those engaged in such work reveals deep dissatisfaction with the inhumane expectations of bureaucrats. Yet effective organizations now recognize the benefits of holistic approaches, treating people and issues as interrelated parts of a field. The complexity of the world is now such that no one person or even small group can alone determine strategy, control or lead. Knowing how to distribute the responsibility and motivation of each different participant is a defining characteristic of leadership. The aim of such leadership is not to be at the centre of performance but, almost invisibly, to enhance the sense of well-being, coordinate individuals, groups and the organization as a whole to achieve a mutually beneficial outcome 'that occurs when a leader creates *resonance* – a reservoir of positivity that frees the best in people. At its root, then, the primal job of leadership is emotional' (Goleman, Boyatzis and McKee, 2002, p. ix).

Leadership and management

A leader expresses the will of people and leaves them better off (cf. Grint, 1995, p. 127). Taking responsibility for general performance and the achievement of objectives is a management function:

> The manager administers; the leader innovates . . . the manager has his or her eye on the bottom line; the leader has his or her eye on the horizon . . . the manager maintains, the leader develops . . . the manager asks how and when; the leader asks what and why. (Church, quoting Bennis, in Bennis, Spreitzer and Cummings, 2001, p. 222)

Zaleznik (1998), in common with a number of management writers, also differentiates the leader from the manager. The similar, stereotypical view of Genevieve Capowski (1994) sets out a contrast between visionary/rational, passionate/consulting and creative/persistent. The prominent theorist John P. Kotter insists that managers need to know when and how to lead (Dubrin, 2001, p. 4). In reality, the difference between management and leadership is one of emphasis and overlapping roles. Effective leaders also manage, and effective managers also lead. Cammock analyses the manager's responsibilities through three sub-roles: technical, management and leadership. Although some managers are practically involved in every aspect of a project, generally, senior managers engage others for the technical operational tasks. Managers bring order and consistency to efficient working practice. Certainly, as Bennis analyses, leaders innovate while management imitates, but there also comes a point when managers exercise the purposeful forms of leadership that bring about change. Equally, leaders who take no interest in day-to-day stability, or who will not act in partnership with those concerned with deadlines and budgets, run a serious risk of derailing an organization. Costly mistakes are made through inappropriate appointments to key positions. Group evaluation systems exist to enable organizations to identify potential leaders for the inter-personal, conceptual or strategic skills in which they are strong and which the organization requires at a particular moment in its history. Pivotal roles can be designed so that, supported by develop-ment programmes, people can succeed, with the recognition of leadership as

> a complex, multifaceted capability, with myriad nuances and subtleties and that the characteristics that can help a person succeed in one environment (turning round a losing division for instance) may lead to failure in another situation (such as starting up a new business). (Sorcher and Brant, 2002, p. 78)

Adaptive working

Mobilizing organizations to make critical behavioural change is a key leadership role. Moving beyond problem solving and through the painful learning of new behaviours, adaptive work happens when

> deeply held beliefs are challenged, when the values that made us successful become less relevant, and when legitimate, yet competing perspectives emerge. Often the toughest task for leaders in effecting change is mobilizing people throughout the organization to do adaptive work. (Heifetz and Laurie, 1997, p. 124)

In contrast to many of the earlier theories and practice, ideas about adaptive organizations seek a more integrated, holistic approach to challenges. Bolman and Deal expose the simplistic analysis of lead-ership 'universally offered as a panacea for almost any social problem' (Bolman and Deal, 2003b, p. 86). The team leader's leader-ship consists in knowing how to shape and draw out the leadership of all the constituent members in their authority, energy, capability and capacity. So, while solo leadership cannot rescue any organiza-tion, it has a fundamental part to play in determining both the direction and the way in which change occurs. Effective leadership critically draws all parts of the organization to cooperate in a productive manner, unlocking the potential of individuals and showing them ways to work together and individually for a synergistic outcome for the organization. In this sense leadership throughout the many levels of an organization is a 'field of interaction' (Boyett and Boyett, 1998, p. 14).

Diffidence is often expressed at the suggestion that the Church may have anything in common with an aggressive, marketing-led production company. In Chapter 4 we explored the dangers for people and institutions when their unconscious aggression is denied. We have also just highlighted the dangers of visionary leadership that underplays the tasks of management. As we observed in Chapter 3, trinitarian, mission-focused ecclesiology and organizational theory have a particular opportunity for dialogue when public power relationships are conceived in terms of the learning community. In serving a need within the mess and chaos of a particular environment, the learning community grows and changes, without the self-limiting expectation of neat and rapid solutions. In situations of very different scales, this learning model has the potential to draw together humanistic and theological models of people working towards a common vision. The adaptive organization model, building on the work of Senge and others, is rooted in the necessity for and talent of leaders to perceive what is required in terms of task and interpersonal factors in widely different environments.

Adaptive organizations are characterized by openness, willingness to accept risk and an entrepreneurial outlook (Deal and Kennedy, 2000, p. 30). While organizations, generally, are capable of displaying these characteristics occasionally, adaptive organizations purposively pursue these behaviours as core values. External changes (in societies, markets and technology globally), beyond the control of the organization, are accepted as positive challenges for clarifying values and discovering new ways of functioning. In such circumstances the work of leadership is to encourage people to do adaptive work.

In traditional organizations, managers and leaders distinctively protect 'their people' from harsh external realities. It has been the norm within the business culture for individual employees not to deal directly with external pressures. Earlier we explored the normal response to external crisis: restructuring, downsizing or otherwise making technical changes to the functioning of the organization.

Traditionally, employees are the recipients of hierarchical management decisions.

Despite the much-prized autonomy of local clergy and churches, a similar top-down process is a familiar response to external challenges with mainline churches. The Diocese of Texas, in its restructuring for mission in the twenty-first century, notes that the Church is subject to similar forces to those battering other organizations: rapid technological change, greater 'consumer' diversity, demands for improved service quality and greater competence, increased competition, information explosion and overload, dramatic demographic changes, and in terms of church membership, shrinking 'market share'. The diocese believes the hierarchical model of maintenance to be not only ineffective, but a threat to organizational survival (Payne and Beazley, 2001, pp. 74ff).

Policy documents of mainline Churches in the UK regularly speak eloquently of the Church as one body and as modelling itself on the *koinonia* associated with trinitarian-shaped patterns of power. However, separated from theology, pragmatic planning to deal with financial and statistical crises reveals all the hallmarks of anxious, secretive, top-down, and benign but patronizing, pyramidical organizational patterns. Parallel with changes in universities and hospitals, church managers are accepting that they can no longer guarantee jobs for life. Creatively, in the Church in Wales, instead of labelling clergy from the point of selection for ordination training as 'stipendiary' or 'non-stipendiary', terms with limited value perhaps for church accountants, the bishops propose a more flexible policy. The church will ordain some priests and deacons with the likelihood that their ministry will contain a degree of oversight of the work of others and some whose ministry is likely to be very locally rooted. Vacant posts will be advertised as attracting a full, part or no stipend. It is certainly likely that the posts attracting a full stipend and house will be more likely to require the skills and attitudes of oversight, and to that extent, some clergy are more likely than others to be appointed to 'stipendiary' posts. Experience and reflection often bring maturity and so, at different stages in life, priests and deacons may well be called to a variety of forms of ministry.

The expectation of the bishops is that clergy will eventually stop considering themselves as fixed permanently in one track or the other and that, in the future, there can be no guaranteed income or pension for a working life. Although reflecting much more the realities of work in the wider world, this development, while increasing the flexibility of the church overall, removes the peace of mind and emotional stability associated with Anglican clergy. For Anglican churches, with a distinctive Benedictine inheritance, the shock to the culture is profound when financial realities mean that a place can no longer be guaranteed for everyone regardless of their skill or attitude to the corporate enterprise. This impacts too on the discussion in Chapter 4 of the archetypical work that clergy perform for Church and society. It seems important here also to lament the incalculable loss of familiar forms. The long-practised response to external threat, in this case new financial realities, is to make structural decisions that can result in the amputation of large parts of the organization. The result, as we have discussed in previous chapters, is not just a loss of people but a seismic increase in anxiety and a deep resentment or cynicism among those remaining. Adaptive organizational practice is more likely to serve the Church than previous models of power.

The notion that it is appropriate for leaders of organizations to insulate 'their people' from the realities of outside threats must be challenged. All the members of the organization need to offer their emotional intelligence to meeting the challenge of an external force. This requires significant cultural change, for two reasons. First, leaders with higher status generally feel responsible for making decisions themselves. Adopting a less directive and authoritative approach can raise distress levels in both leader and led. Secondly, employees and volunteers within an organization generally expect leaders (with higher status and pay) to carry the burden of decision making, relieving them of responsibility. For organizations to become adaptive, the expectation that leaders will make all the decisions and that followers will be passive and relieved of the burden has to be 'unlearned' (Heifitz and Laurie, 1997, p. 171). The need to unlearn this culture is vital within the Church where, through patterns of mutual collusion, laity disempower themselves and clergy come to believe in the inevitability of overwork and of holding themselves so personally responsible as to distort power relations within the Church as a whole. Inevitably this raises the question as to how destructive of equal expectation is the structure of pay differentials (rather than adequate expenses) for such posts as archdeacon and bishop.

A consensus emerges that organizations are more likely to flourish through adapting when individuals regard themselves as 'agents':

> we find the ethical responsibility for the 'health' or good of the system focused on the commitment and caring of the individual. This is even clearer in the theory of complex adaptive systems because of its focus on the agents. If the individual is considered to be the agent, this agent is also considered to have rational powers of thought and freedom of choice. (Griffin, 2002, p. 76)

It is the coming together of a number of individuals who 'care' and who are prepared to act that gives adaptive systems their strength. While the individual in an adaptive system may be autonomous, it is the collective actions of those individuals who 'care' that determine the culture that emerges (ibid., pp. 77ff).

Adaptive leadership

Adaptive organizations recognize the immense variety of leadership models and how at different stages in the life of organizations differing patterns will be required: 'Defining leadership is a generational endeavour. While the traits and attributes can be timeless, each generation has to filter the meaning through its own experience and collective anchors' (Headington in Bennis, Spreitzer and Cummings, 2001, p. 228).

A leader's performance produces contrasting responses in different people and environments. Hugh recalls a manager with a reputation for being 'old-fashioned', operating a culture of fear and of disparagement of those he did not understand. He was short on praise and long on criticism. Many who worked 'under' him felt devalued and discouraged and would not have described him as a 'good' manager. He assisted the company to achieve high results in economic terms but at a high human cost. Respected by the senior management, focused principally on economic returns, his over-forceful style disaffected others. Whereas any organizational leadership that produces negative emotions in workers, such as chronic anger, stress, or a sense of futility, cannot be praised, there are important contextual issues to be addressed.

Contextual definition is critical to understanding leadership, but nothing remains immutable: the definition has to be revisited periodically to ensure its continuing validity for that place and time. Rather than dealing in absolutes about leaders, adaptive theory, against the specifics of the organization, asks, 'Does the leader contribute towards achieving the mission of this organization?'; 'How much?'; 'Is this leader attuned to the culture and behavioural norms of the organization or do they "do their own thing"?'

In traditional organizations, based on top-down power and boundaries, such questions may appear fatuous. However, a distinction has to be made between a leader who is effective and one who is simply efficient. Efficiency is doing the thing right, but effectiveness is doing the right things (Drucker, 1977, p. 44). In conventional organizations leaders may normally be authoritative and directive. These are preferred characteristics for some employees: 'Tell me what I need to do, to meet your (i.e. the organization's) objectives!' In such a response lies apparent safety. By contrast, the behaviours of leaders and employees in adaptive organizations may be quite different and sometimes appear anarchic to the outsider.

The training of a military or police officer today is not a matter of learning set procedures for all occasions. Rather the training educates the recruit in three ways simultaneously: first, to know the values and tradition of the army or the police force and the freedoms and constraints offered by the aim of a planned operation; second, to know how to read with speed and accuracy the particulars of any given situation; and third, how to make an emotionally intelligent connection between them. It would be on the quality of that connection that leadership would be assessed. Knowing how to judge the vital priorities in each moment is what distinguishes 'effective' leadership. Such issues must similarly be of importance in the training and regular review of clergy.

Adaptive organizations actively encourage leadership behaviours that in more traditional organizations might be regarded as destructive. An illustration of this is dissent. In more traditional hierarchical organizations, dissent or open criticism are considered as intolerable threats to the leadership (authority) of the organization. In adaptive cultures it is recognized that, given the right cultural conditions, employees intend the best for the organization and their critique may be assumed to be constructive. Those who criticize or challenge either the status quo or future proposals do so for the common good. The fear that criticism is personally or organization-ally corrosive is not part of adaptive working, which proactively develops a culture thriving on fast response and self-critique as the natural stimulus for improved performance. Where control is main-tained primarily through the exercise of top-down authority, certain human personalities make difficulties for leaders and managers. Those who prove 'difficult' are removed as too costly in terms of management energy. In Belbin's theories, the 'Plant', especially intelligent, assertive and gifted at generating new ideas, will sit light to protocols and can be a prickly character. In terms of team per-formance, however, the Plant lies slightly ahead of the other roles, along with the balancing 'Company Worker', combining reliability, caution and common sense (Belbin, 1996a, pp. 74, 119).

Developing adaptive leadership

Leaders need to be aware of and include within their repertoire some competency in four kinds of response to contextual challenge (cf. Bolman and Deal, 2003b, pp. 86ff).

1 Structural leadership

In some respects structural leadership appears to be a conventional response to external challenges, unrelated to mutual or dynamic concepts of power. The principal focus of structural leadership is design of the organization to handle the particular challenges it faces. The most frequent response to a changing situation, often followed by churches, is to redesign the way things are done or radically to reshape structures and personnel. As structural leader-ship concentrates primarily on the organization rather than on the people, charismatic style and communication with colleagues are a low priority. Leaders, according to this perspective, respond to the organizational challenge by developing new strategies:

> It is leadership's responsibility to create a strategy that will cause the organization to succeed, to grow, to prosper, to beat the competition. In a borderless economy, the question 'What is our strategy and what are our competitors' strategies?' must, like the question 'What is our core business?' be raised and answered often because the strategy has to derive from the competitive reality of the business. (J. M. Bardwick in Hessel-bein *et al.*, 1996, p. 135)

Strategy is not the only priority for a leader, but developing a 'winning strategy' is a key leadership function. Essentially, this is a structural approach. For the structural leader, the logic is clear: define and communicate the strategy and the organization will follow. This is very much a top-down, authority-led approach. Bardwick's views on strategy derive from her assertion that 'the most important question in any organization has to be, "What is the business of our business?"' (ibid., p. 134).

Church responses to such questions as 'Why are we here? Why are we using these resources in this particular way?' vary considerably. In their deceptive simplicity the questions highlight an undeniable challenge for all Church leaders. Without effective answers that enjoy broad acceptance and commitment, the prospects for the development of any church must be limited. An understanding of common purpose in the light of the realities of the current situation is critical.

The Church's authority is dissipated when its character and manner of operating are not a chosen enactment of its purpose to be an advance sign of the coming reign of God. A vital element of a gospel community is to be open to the radical demands of the active life of God in praise and thanksgiving, to 'participate in the movement of God's truth towards human beings, a directed openness' (Hardy, 1996, pp. 5–6). The Acts of the Apostles epitomizes how church leadership is intimately connected with worship. 'Key decisions and key visions for leadership typically come out of a context of worship. Mission and social action both seem to flow from worship' (Gill and Burke, 1996, p. 5).

While the form of worship may vary widely, worship in itself, the leading of it and the formal coming together, is in considerable part a structural activity, part of the ritual of the Church, but it also echoes elements of the three leadership types we discuss below. As such it makes a vital link between theology, church practice and adaptive culture theories.

Bardwick argues that successful companies have knowledge not only of 'our' strategy, but also of the strategy of 'our competitors'. How could a church relate to that? In the earlier discussion of repressed shadows (see Chapter 4), we acknowledged the Church's unexpressed aggression. In examining a general apathy towards ecumenism, we noted the understated but real competitive spirit between denominations locally. Who are the 'competitors'? Is this a meaningful question to consider in a church context? The size of congregations is not, in absolute terms, 'the business of our business', yet the absence of people from a congregation is at least a vital question to consider both locally and on the wider cultural canvas of religious belief and cultural change:

> In the context of over a century of churchgoing decline in Britain, we too believe that numbers are important . . . both a quantitative and qualitative concern about churchgoing should be a major priority for British church leaders today. Strategic leadership does make an attempt, wherever possible, to measure and assess outcomes against stated objectives as accurately and truthfully as possible. A frequent sign of ineffective leadership is a tendency either to ignore or to excuse actual outcomes and accountability. Audit is an essential tool of strategic leadership. (Gill and Burke, 1996, p. 11)

We add the important rider, in the spirit of Martin Luther King Jr's interrogative, 'Who is their God?', that the mere existence of a robust congregation is not sufficient evidence of 'success'.

As we have seen, structural leaders do not need to be charismatic, as their strength lies in detailed observation of the context and in rethinking the relationship between that and the organization's structure and strategy. Structural leaders also focus very heavily on implementation, using process to override resistance with a consequent tendency to neglect personal needs. Finally, structural leaders experiment, evaluate and adapt. This is very much the implication of Gill and Burke's approach to church leadership, based on measurement and audit. As circumstances change, structures must be modified. Concisely, structural leaders focus on the method and shape of the organization. In the church context, such activity is recognizable in the adjustment of structures, the rebalancing of powers between different governing bodies, and over time the shifting of responsibility, for example for financial liabilities or educational provision, from province to diocese or to deanery and then back again in the light of experience.

Organizations are structures or, better, fields, that are constantly evolving. Structural leadership contributes to the adaptive organization when the impetus for change comes, not from the top or centre as in a traditional organization, but from groups of individuals or 'sub-cultures' (Deal and Kennedy, 2000, pp. 213ff). Leadership in adaptive cultures happens anywhere and at any time. In traditional cultures, delegated authority can be mapped directly from the top, but in adaptive cultures the means are subtler. It is the norms and values defining of the organization, rather than regulations, that authorize the actions of individuals and sub-cultures.

2 Human resource leadership

Human resource leadership, far less directive in approach than structural leadership, describes leaders as 'enablers' or 'facilitators', focusing on helping others to achieve. It is easier to see how the approach of human resource leadership might initially, at least in comparison to structural leadership, be viewed as the archetypal adaptive form. Its concentration on openness, listening, coaching and participation highlights an approach that supports adaptivity.

The Christian management consultant Robert Greenleaf, for whom Jesus is the exemplar, has developed the concept of servant leadership. Distancing himself from hierarchical management, Greenleaf advocates leadership as service. When service is the key, the willingness of people to participate in a spirit of mutual trust and loyalty becomes evident: 'those who report to the servant-leader, are empowered, grow in confidence, achieve greater autonomy, and are more likely to become servant-leaders themselves' (Payne and Beazley, 2001, p. 75).

Patterns of collaborative ministry arise from a renewed emphasis on baptismal call to service, echoing Christ's serving of the Father's mission. Servants are not concerned about being served (Luke 17.7–10; Matthew 20.26–8); are no greater than their master (John 15.20; Matthew 10.24), to whom they are wholeheartedly devoted (Luke 16.13); work for the master's coming (Matthew 24.45–6); are unconcerned at impressing others (Galatians 1.10; Ephesians 6.6), and are promoted to greater responsibility through showing faithfulness in small matters (Matthew 24.20–1).

Jesus' negation of the leadership modelled by the Gentiles of his day has continually emerging consequences, as successive generations of church aspire to becoming the kind of community that is Spirit-led and Christ-shaped. A corrective to a naïve approach to collaborative ministry is the recognition that some tasks in the church can only be discharged by commissioned leadership. Workshops on this topic usually disagree on the precise list of what only some can do and what would constitute a dereliction of duty. We accept the principle, despite a deep unease with the verb 'to delegate' in church matters. There are certain givens about the task of the nominated one in charge, but when the baptized and baptizing people of God find their place in God's mission, either specifically for building the Church or else the Kingdom in the world, it is from a power given to each as of right by the Holy Spirit. However, Higginson, reflecting on the self-denial of a former governor of Judah (Nehemiah 5.14–19), rightly encourages leaders to be willing to accept pay cuts or to forgo privileges associated with high office to reduce the burdens of others.

Organizational consultants have expanded the potential of servant leadership for unlocking the energy of others (Bolman and Deal, 2003b, p. 98). For example, Edward Headington, reminiscent of the practice of Vincent Donovan among the Masai, reflects that the true leader will not attempt to take us to the place we used to be nor to where he or she is. Rather, 'The servant leaders of the future will take us to places we have never gone before as polity; perhaps by recognizing that we must be the change we wish to see in the world, we can lead by example' (Headington in Bennis, Spreitzer and Cummings, 2001, p. 237; see Donovan, 1982).

To summarize, human resource leadership supports people through communicating and encouraging their productive living out of their belief. Such leaders are accessible, respecting the potential of the partnership with each person in the organization (Peters, 1995).

3 Political leadership

Political leaders focus on *what* needs to be achieved but see the method in behavioural terms (Kouzes, 2003, p. 101). They need to be clearer about their goals than those preferring other approaches, since their methods of persuasion, their principal resource in achieving their goals, have the potential to become manipulative. What is at issue is the human maturity of the leader as a person. However clear the understanding of the goal, this is essentially a very pragmatic style but, while political leaders have a very clear understanding of what they want to achieve, this is balanced with a deep appreciation of what is achievable in practice. The methods used to achieve goals depend contingently on the particular people and situation.

The approach depends on an understanding of the ability of people to access their power and to know their intentions. Motivational theories pioneered by Maslow regard the structure of the human person as a psychological organism seeking its full potential. Organizational psychologists have not been slow to understand the benefits of combining the desired outcome of business with the enrichment of employees 'as an alternative to the excessively narrow, authoritarian, and dehumanizing work orientation generated by scientific management and classical management theory' (Morgan, 1997, p. 36).

A repertoire of organizational possibilities emerges. Cynically one can recognize how business might hope to offer employees a 'higher level' work environment without increasing financial liability, though the real loss of organizational power resulting from ignoring the social dimension of work is now exposed. Since the 1990s business systems have increasingly aspired to effectiveness through recognizing social, cultural and political modes of resistance (ibid., p. 39). Political leaders assess needs and interests but also power bases. Who, internally and externally, has influential power? The political leader will target those people for particular phased attention: to influence, persuade, negotiate and sometimes coerce.

Leaders function not only within but also at the edges of organizations: they are the eyes and ears of the organization, watching the outside world and identifying external threats and opportunities. Equally they are the mouth of the organization, representing it to the world. No amount of structural or human resource leadership can mitigate external forces; this is the forte of the political leader.

The language used of Christian ministry increasingly includes the concepts of overseeing, presiding or episcope, locally and regionally. A general expectation in the modern Church is that leaders have only three possible strategies for change: influence, negotiation or persuasion. At the conscious level, coercion conjures up notions of power that belong to former, less enlightened times. However, we would argue that within the presiding model, although permission giving and praise are vital, so is the setting down of markers. Occasionally the leader has to say, on the community's behalf, 'this is unacceptable power abuse', 'we cannot support you in this strategy or treatment of others', or 'we believe the consequences will be destructive of any recognizable notion of church'. Having the discernment to know when that is must be one of the gifts that identify those with both the capability and the capacity for overseeing.

The difficult and stretching reflections on the very 'personal' life of a bishop by Penny Jamieson offer a reminder of the world's desperate need of gospel forms of power, and the tough personal implications for those who are charged sometimes to make decisions for the sake of the many. We have earlier explored the need for leaders to be representatives, willing to live with ambivalence, modelling non-abusive power, and building up the Church's identity in the embraced, crucified vulnerability of Jesus (Jamieson, 1997, pp. 8ff). Jamieson expresses concern at the possibility that the Church might take too much notice of organizational theory about the achievement of goals. However, her articulation of a concept of sacramental leadership, built on a thoroughly relational ecclesiology, politically combines purpose with people. The one who leads, in every respect, public and private, is one who can offer an integrated path along which the purpose and method of the Church can be advanced. To maintain the Church in its identity requires a deep focusing on God in worship, prayer and study. The church leader has to learn when to relax formalities (about local ecumenical practice, for example) and when to engage with tough intentionality and courteously, to help the Church constantly to re-find its character and purpose. Facing and managing conflict cannot be avoided but the quality of such encounters can either distract the Church or promote its task of showing the world its true life.

As we have suggested, political leadership is easily misconstrued in a world in which people have become politically astute, scanning public leaders' every word for hidden nuance and meaning. Leaders who are most comfortable with this style have to recognize the sophisticated personalities of organizational participants and use every opportunity for training and supervision in becoming ever more adept at their task.

4 Symbolic leadership

Symbolic leadership is likely to be the pattern that resonates most immediately for the Church, based as it is in tradition and storytelling. This approach believes organizations find their deepest meaning in interpreting and reinterpreting familiar, lingering, prophetic voices and texts. Tom Peters, although a popularist exponent of human resources leadership, also personally models the symbolic leader role. His management, leadership and organizational development studies rely on stories designed not only to illustrate his points but also to encourage others to imitate leaders of earlier times (Peters, 1995, pp. 183ff).

Texts and stories are re-employed in fresh situations to assist a new generation to make meaning of its life with God. Strong rereadings contribute to courageous acts of interpretation. For example, Martin Luther takes a text from Isaiah (5.20) and turns the prophet into a 'theologian of the cross'. The verse that was originally a critique of ungodly ideas and ways of living becomes a Christian theological statement. What for Isaiah was evil, for Luther is the opposite of the scandalous way of the cross (Brueggemann, 2000, p. 23). This is not a matter of correcting the past but of allowing for the intuitive transformation of human society now by the process of rereading a text rooted in the holiness of God.

The Gospels and Paul speak of response to Jesus' call in terms of risk to be both personally chosen and also disregarded – living as the flowers of the field, leaving the dead to bury their dead. Metz comments that with the notable exceptions of various liberation theologies, churches and leaders evade this dangerous memory of Jesus, not through naïveté, but through the contagious diseases of banality and fear that lead to powerlessness (Downey, 1999, pp. 143ff). Peter on the day of Pentecost repeatedly inspires the Church in ever new situations to be free, bold and hopeful in disciple-making:

> What a stunning vocation for the Church, to stand free and hope-filled in a world gone fearful . . . and to think, imagine, dream, vision a future that God will yet enact. What a work of visioning for the Church when society all around is paralysed in fear, preoccupied by commodity, mesmerized by wealth, seeking endless power, and deeply, deeply, frightened. (Florence, 2004, p. 115; see also Payne and Beazley, 2001, p. 192)

Symbolic leadership emphasizes that communicating a vision requires credibility in the communicator. John P. Kotter suggests that able leaders come from the ranks of those who, in their early adulthood, were riskily trusted with leadership opportunities and time for reflection. A key element in Kotter's analysis of successfully communicating a vision is the need for leadership by example (Boyett and Boyett, 1998, pp. 41–2, 62–3). The meaning of symbols needs to be readily available. Symbolic leaders constantly use and reinterpret images to encourage and inform others.

Symbolic communication requires memorable pictures that evoke deep resonances. The gifts of rhetoric, oratory, speech making and preaching can elevate communication to an almost mystical relationship between speaker and audience, a connective field uniting leaders and followers. Compelling communication becomes dialogical as the response of the hearers feeds back naturally to the speaker. However, integrity and authenticity are ultimately the most powerful communicators of all (Cammock, 2003, p. 53).

The sharply contrasting hyper-connectedness and schisms of current society demand leaders who understand and live up to the holistic nature of leadership. Cammock encourages leaders to increase their skills of envisioning, engaging and enacting. The envisioning task of leadership demands the shaping of a shared purpose through sensing opportunity or recognizing the need for change, establishing direction and awakening and creating a sense of urgency. Engaging and enacting involve the abilities of communication, enlisting others, articulation and achieving the vision, and aligning, motivating, inspiring and encouraging people (ibid., p. 41). Developing, relating and embodying a story is the gift of the innovative leader, who, like a brilliant stand-up comedian or preacher

> develops a story that is already latent in his or her social context and brings it forward with a fresh twist that captures the imaginations of his or her followers. The 'rarest individual' is the visionary leader [who] actually creates a new story, one not known to most individuals before . . . Moses, Confucius, Christ, and Gandhi are examples of such visionary leaders. The first task is *developing a story*. The second is the *relating of the story*, achieved by various forms of communication and by the actual embodiment of the story in terms of the leader's own life. (ibid., p. 40)

Adaptive leaders depend on stories to provide answers to questions such as 'Who are we?', 'Where have we come from?', 'Where are we now?', and 'Where are we going?' Such story-telling relates to the identity, not merely of the organization, but of the persons constituting the organization. Emotional involvement and commitment matures as individuals strongly identify with common core values of the organization. For the Church, biblical stories and parables interpreted in terms of current situations traditionally form the foundation for understanding. However, all organizations, including the Church, find that positive stories of success, of overcoming difficulties, of boldness, leadership or self-sacrifice can encourage others to recognize their own capacity and capability. The experience of building up a new small congregation, or the group that meets a sharp but previously unrecognized social need, may present the values that will inspire others to tackle problems in their own particular situation.

It is in the area of story-telling that Tom Peters provides the greatest illustration of his own effective leadership. His strength lies in the ability to understand ideas and to map, distil and communicate their power, illustrating with infinite stories. Storytellers are pivotal to the development of corporate cultures as they interpret events and create corporate myths that reinforce core values, resonate with the corporate culture, demonstrate what is important in the organization and give meaning to the mundane (Deal and Kennedy, 2000, p. 9).

Effective leaders demonstrate *resonance* with those they lead. This is more than empathy, but is the ability to engage the emotional energy of others and form bonds between group members. The resonant leader also interprets and re-presents the emotions of the group, reinforcing 'synchrony just as much as enthusiasm does, because it leaves people feeling understood and cared for' (Goleman, Boyatzis and McKee, 2002, p. 20). The power of story-telling is a vital means by which to reinforce culture. The most effective stories are those that are constantly retold, building on and reinforcing the previous wealth of story (Boyett and Boyett, 1998, p. 31). The real power of the story comes in the constant informal retelling, for it is through this process that the meanings become interwoven with the fabric of the organization.

Challenges for the Church

Adaptive leadership in situations of flux requires leaders not only to understand the contrasting styles that may need to be employed but also to be able to know which form of leadership to adopt in the face of specific challenges. We have already accumulated a sense of the major issues currently facing leaders, locally and regionally, in the Church. The capacity to balance stability with the development of a vision for the contemporary Church in society, requires leadership that can remain vulnerable through a deepening holiness, and can collaborate with others in the formation of culture, values and detailed planning. Leaders also need the personal maturity and skill to manage controversy. Church leaders need to be growing in self-knowledge in order to recognize and critique the archetypes laid upon them. To be constantly the focus of unrealistic expectations and often scapegoated for corporate issues, requires every leader to take support (spiritual direction and therapeutic work supervision) to track their part in the power dynamics of the 'field' of which they are a pivotal part. All leaders should recognize their need of support in assessing how much work is required to perform their job creatively. This includes the practice of greater fluidity and the skills of motivating others. Senior leaders in the Church also have to be creative in balancing time-consuming pastoral care and disciplinary issues with the discernment of what is required in their role in parishes, the diocese, secular structures and the wider Church. 'Church leaders . . . need to move away from an incremental and consensus style of leadership. A more strategic understanding of both budgets and decision making is imperative' (Gill and Burke, 1996, p. 75).

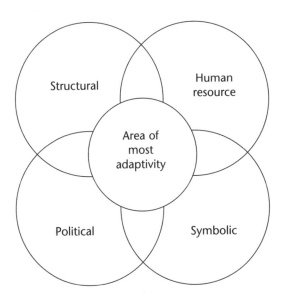

Leaders can only exist in a context where others are prepared to follow. In a business context the awkward term 'followership' is used to a considerable extent, though not entirely, to refer to the cash nexus between organization and employee. Those who fail to follow or conform eventually cease to be employees. The link weakens in an environment where groups of employees exercise particular power through the ability to bargain collectively, due to a shortage of their particular skills or as a result of easier external employment conditions.

This causes severe problems for the Church. 'Followers', characteristically the 'ordinary lay person', exercise extraordinary power: have free will to remain or to go. The chief response of dioceses is to talk the language of theology and purpose but then merely to alter structures, often in the light of organizational theory that has already been superseded or has little resonance with a Christian theology of God or of human relationships.

Robin recalls how a diocese once placed its central resource team in the hands of external reviewers. The review team was comprised of early-retired managers from industry who, although they were regular worshippers, had had no encouragement or resources in their own local church to check for connections between models of organization espoused in their business life and the meanings to be found in the triune God. There was small wonder that the methods and results of the review of church personnel lacked authority and scored very badly in terms of appreciating the work and engaging with the people concerned.

Drawing from the main themes of this study of power, and with acknowledgement of developments in forms of leadership identified by Boyett and Boyett (1998, pp. 17 ff) we now advocate a number of leadership characteristics for the energizing of people and communities.

1 From strategist to visionary

Robin recalls Rowan Williams' instinctive recoil from the term 'strategy' so far as the Church is concerned. Certainly strategic development in business is linked to a hierarchical approach to leadership. Strategy has been the product of 'senior' leaders and managers, privately, in the higher reaches of the organization and then, with a modicum of discussion, cascaded down. A 'strategic' approach remains highly popular in church development and some degree of strategic leadership is essential in any organization. Theorists now recognize, however, that strategy is not sufficient to mobilize or motivate people in a culture in which 'freedom' and 'rights' are better understood and more widely pursued than in any previous generation. Since the pivotal work on ecclesiology and ministry of Edward Schillebeeckx in the 1980s, we have remembered that all ministry finds its necessary authority through interconnectedness. No one possesses a ministry in isolation or that is permanently super- or sub-ordinate. It was the wisdom of Leon Joseph Suenens that the role of the one in charge is to draw out, coordinate and sustain the entire Church's ministry. Daniel Hardy has consistently shown how the Church loses the circle of its authority when both parties collude in perpetuating the myth that clerical experts may supplant the vocation of every Christian. Theologically, the Church's alternative practice of community, as an evangelical witness to society, assumes that all participate in the holiness and liveliness of the triune God. Patterns of mutual relatedness, patience and service are the Christian context for effective leadership. The Church has naturally borrowed the term 'strategy' in its attempts in the last few decades to make coherent plans, involving every dimension of a diocese or regional organization, and to work them through. However, just as the notion of 'field theory' has more synergy than 'systems theory', the Church needs now to abandon talk of 'strategy' in favour of 'vision': 'People aren't engaged by strategies. They don't form any strong emotional attachment to them. Strategies answer *what* but don't answer *why*, and knowing why is more important' (Boyett and Boyett, 1998, p. 18).

In a factory where the pace and nature of the work is controlled largely by the process, there is a greater tendency to treat people as part of the machine, to be directed to meet the needs and limitations of the technology. However, as education has improved and with the demise of coal-stack industries, an ever greater proportion of the population are 'knowledge-workers' (Handy, [1989] 1990, pp. 82–7). This change reflects the greater movements in society that we have already highlighted and is both symptom and cause of a greater questioning of all types of authority, one that reinforces the need to involve people emotionally with change. As we discussed in terms of learning organization theory, answering the *why* question is central.

The emotional engagement by 'resonant' leaders of employees, throughout the company, is fundamental in producing exceptional results, particularly in organizations that rely on service. Self-directed learning and the discovery of the true self can create the necessary leadership for organizations that intend to work on trust and mutual regard (Goleman, Boyatzis and McKee, 2002, pp. 91ff):

> I don't believe top management should be in the business of strategy setting at all, except as creators of a general business mission. Strategies must be set from below. (No, not 'from' below. Set 'in' below – i.e., by the autonomous business units, for the autonomous business units. And 'below' is all wrong, too . . . damnable words!). (Peters, 1992, p. 13)

Church leaders must learn that people respond most effectively when it is clear, in practice, that everyone together, in their complementary roles and with their particular expertise, is part of the discernment and decision-making process. The role of effective leadership is to describe the overall purpose, the objectives and the vision. One of the leader's primary roles is visionary. It is the prophetic role that in various ways we have been exploring in scripture, spirituality and theories of human relating.

Luke describes the intentional practice of Christian community living in terms of sociology, 'a decisive energizing towards a new social reality' (Brueggemann, 1978, p. 97). Luke presents his protest in the song of the angels and the song of Mary. Jesus' ministry among us is bound to lead to energizing new possibilities as an astonishing and troubling gift from God. To exercise prophetic leadership is to move beyond the 'Royal Consciousness' that marginalizes, silences and binds. Out of darkness, we are called to self-awareness and self-actualization so that we can be with people really and honestly. We hardly know, even in the Church, how to let go of the false self. Now is a time for grieving the loss of what the Church has failed to be, especially for those who live without meaning. We need to grieve for all that we have not been, in the hope that the joyful responsibility of which Jesus was God's primary enactment, may come alive among us for the world's repairing. 'We are at the edge of knowing this in our personal lives, for we understand a bit of the processes of grieving. But we have yet to learn and apply it to the reality of society' (ibid., p. 113).

We need church leaders who are expected to challenge the dominant myths and generate unorthodox ideas that destabilize the organization in a controlled and deliberate new way. 'Primal Leadership' is the painting of mind pictures, capable of engaging the emotional interest of their followers (Goleman, Boyatzis and McKee, 2002, ch. 1). This leadership does not answer the *why* question separately or directly, but indirectly it demonstrates clearly that action is required to reach this new vision together:

> No matter what leaders set out to do – whether it's creating strategy or mobilizing teams to action – their success depends on *how* they do it. Even if they get everything else just right, if leaders fail in this primal task of driving emotions in the right direction, nothing they do will work as well as it could or should. (ibid., p. 3)

The Church should embrace current expectations that leaders will bring a strong ethical dimension into the forming of effective organizations. This is not simply a question of morality, although this is part of the question, but rather one of the development of values that form a unique culture. Where visionary leadership is strong, the organization's character reflects the value systems of its leaders, resulting in performance raised to truly extraordinary levels (Deal and Kennedy, 2000, p. 211).

In different but complementary ways, a whole host of the theologians with whom we have engaged are advocating a Church intentionally shaped as a reading of the gospel in all its relations, internal and external. The current sharp and unity-threatening international Anglican debate on biblical authority and sexual identity acts as a warning against the possibility of a naïve consensus on the nature and values of Christian community. However, we believe a deep implication of our study is that a Church that is conscious of having a vital role to perform for the world's well-being constantly re-finds itself, in infinite localities, within a structured chaos. Indeed the gospel gives core values and norms of practice; church is discernible as distinctive and yet it cannot afford the luxury of a pretended purity or of remaining in isolated indifference to the pains of society (Biggar in Nation and Wells, 2000, pp. 141ff).

Vision is not simply the abstract definition of some future ideal, but also involves the practical working out of that ideal in a way that is consistent for the organization as a whole. This contrasts with an authoritarian concept of power, as it requires the positive and consistent engagement of the majority of those in the organization. Paradoxically, as leaders are often the non-conformists, if they are to be found at all levels of the organization, initiating or encouraging change, a unanimous agreement of the entire organization on any key decision is most improbable. By their very nature, fields of activity are events in which constantly interacting and turbulent figures form and then dissolve, making way for others (Bohm, 1995; Perls, Hefferline and Goodman, 1996) A culture that engages people, that allows them to find value and that aids self-actualization, is one in which leadership ceases to consist of the separate development and declamation of strategy. Rather people generate change for themselves to meet their own desired corporate and personal objectives. The role of the leader is to help the people define the culture that works for them.

Adaptive organizations are highly responsive to circumstance but also, for the sake of stability, over time lay down matrices of character. Occasionally a leader makes a tough decision, but it must be consistent with a coherent set of values. 'Peripheral practices come and go. Core values remain constant. This provides the ability to adapt to changing conditions while still maintaining a strong corporate identity' (Deal and Kennedy, 2000, p. 30). Visionary leadership consists in identifying those core values around which members can covenant and, while maintaining and reinforcing these, introduce new ideas and developments that both make sense in the present context and also reinforce the culture.

Research shows the cohesive strength of churches that maintain strict beliefs and rules of acceptable practice (Richter and Francis, 1998, p. 94). However, while 'strictness' may be institutionally advantageous, the theological principles we have espoused prohibit the development of a rigid ecclesiology for the sake of security. In practice, rigidly disciplined organizations tend to be authoritarian and centralized, lacking the high degree of flexibility enabled by self-regulating adaptive cultures that define boundaries rather than strategies and rules. In contrast to those who suggest that leaders begin by envisioning the organization they would like to lead, Boyett and Boyett advocate that leaders should begin by creating the vision and naming the values for their own lives. Where individuals are able to mature anywhere in the organization (through lifelong learning, self-development and so on), the organization is able to become far more dynamic and to capitalize on its latent energy, capability and capacity.

2 From commander to story-teller

In a conversation with a diocesan ministry officer, Robin was told with approval how the new bishop was operating not like his predecessor as head of the family, but with the crispness of an army general. The research of Boyett and Boyett suggests that in an environment in which the wider culture depends largely on emotional involvement and ownership from the 'followers' (who are leaders themselves in some contexts), directive behaviours may not be effective in motivating people to action. In today's society, emotions are more likely to be stirred to resistance in situations where directive behaviours are attempted. The political, human resource and symbolic leadership models described earlier have far more capacity to encourage positive emotional interaction with the organizational aims than do instructions from the top or centre (Richter and Francis, 1998, ch. 9). The Church is not a democracy, nor does it exist merely in intimate communities. However, churches, even those not limited by being 'established', have a marked tendency for self-defeat through choosing to define themselves by way of structures, rules and controls. A basic characteristic of the adaptive organization is a more relaxed and inclusive approach to authority and leadership. However, adaptive organizations, to maintain their identity, require defined and clearly understood systems with explicit core values. Daniel W. Hardy is a leading Anglican exponent of the need for the Church to be the practice of a social life that is a deliberate reading of Christian faith. The Church is a circle of people united through worship, ministry and order, whose purpose is

> to be united in holiness, catholicity and apostolicity. This circle is aided by certain kinds of stimuli: education, ordained ministry, prayerful thought (inquiring ever more profoundly into the life and worship of God in the world). But it is the main task of the people themselves – all who stand in the circle – to make it into a deepening spiral of ever greater participation in the work of God in today's world, which is our vocation as Christians. (Hardy, 1996, p. 219)

Rather than maintain the Church's character and order by rigid rules or dominating authority, adaptive leaders will use creative images and story.

The Jewish and Christian scriptures present God largely through accounts of the experiences of particular people, families, groups, tribes and nations with God. Yahweh is portrayed as artist, king, judge, shepherd, potter, healer, mother, father, gardener, and through many other images none of which are sufficient in themselves. The First Testament stories in Egypt, Babylon and Israel have played a significant part in shaping Western culture. Jesus describes the coming reign of God in terms of people on a journey, losing and finding valuables, employing people, and being reconciled with loved ones. Gospel writers, in their cultural context, reveal the character of Good News from God so that shepherds, women, lepers and terrorists can be among the first to know. The faith of Christians and the identity of the Church is drawn out less by abstract teaching than by stories: of the first missionaries, the desert fathers, Celtic saints, social reformers, spiritual pioneers, those in every generation whose faith survives hardship, persecution and death, and above all those whose lives are clearly possessed by God's Spirit and the cruciform pattern of Jesus' own story.

The Church's ceremonies, rituals and liturgy have the potential power to move through enacting stories of faith via symbol, gesture, movement and speech. Of course, if imagination and courage are lacking, the meaning of such events can be tamed. For example, the normative practice of Maundy Thursday footwashing subtly re-enacts the unconscious patronizing by clergy of a few parishioners with already well-scrubbed feet (Sedmak, 2002, p. 91). Given our strong emphasis on being real and truly ourselves, the personal stories of each church leader, with God and in personal and institutional relations, are a highly significant dimension of the building up or otherwise of the Church's character and dynamic relation to the world. An intimate connection exists between the Church's effectiveness in mission and the quality of sociality (love for God and love for neighbour) revealed through and built up by the everyday stories of our lives with one another, intimately and institutionally.

A modern Christian storyteller, Trevor Dennis, demonstrates powerfully how ancient stories can be retold in an inspirational way for today. His stories often elaborate detail not found in the original, but which reinforces the meaning and connects with the present hearer. In the introduction to *God Treads Softly Here* he writes:

> You might protest, 'But it didn't happen like that!' And I would agree at once, of course, that that is not how the story is told in the Bible. But then I would say, 'Don't worry about it. My story says something else. I'm not trying to compete with the Bible (as if anyone could). I'm simply allowing the storytelling and poetry of the Bible . . . to work on my imagination and my prayer, mixing in my experience and study, and then responding in my own way. That's all.' (Dennis, 2004, p. ix)

Underestimating the power of his own story-telling, Dennis demonstrates the power of evocatively retelling a familiar story, increasing its vitality and potency by adding plausible and memorable detail, so perceiving deeper truths. Another example must surely be Walter Brueggemann. His sermons and prayers assume that God is here in the retelling, challenging identity, nurturing hope, and inviting the hearers in this moment to consider their call. For example, within the liturgy at the beginning of Lent, he retells the story of the voices assailing Jesus in the desert. The tempter speaks not only to Jesus but to the Church. Brueggemann warns against the cunning seeking of the cheap 'magic bread' of outward success in place of a deep trust in the God who invites us to obey and serve rather than to test the God of Moses, of Abraham and Jesus (Brueggemann, 2004, pp. 36–7).

Preachers, poets, artists and musicians in connected but different ways constantly retell the faith narrative, recapitulating its meanings in ever new moments. A fertile source of stories is provided by the many Spirit-led responses to Jesus we call the early Church, what John Polkinghorne imaginatively portrays as 'the background radiation to the Resurrection'. In the retelling, say, of the story of Philip and the Ethiopian Eunuch (Acts 8.26–40), intellect, body and heart are engaged in knowing what this shows us now of human communication, the work of God among us and the character of God's life in the world.

3 From systems architect to change agent and servant

In organizations in which strategy is defined from the top it becomes necessary for leaders and managers to exercise command in order to make the strategy work. However, adaptive organizations have learnt that command and control is an inadequate approach in the absence of an agreed definition of the purpose of the organization and of resonant ways in which people interrelate, personally and structurally, to achieve its purpose. The role of the leader as 'architect' does not imply a pre-drawn design delivered by the expert to the customer. Rather it is the fruit of conversation, e-mail, and text, drawing together purpose, expertise and environment:

> There would be no need to communicate a vision if it were already well-known, widely accepted, and aggressively pursued. People don't need leaders to get them to do what they are already doing. The new leadership is about change, and that is very different from what has gone on in the past. (Boyett and Boyett, 1998, p. 33)

The triune God whose life in the world we have consistently explored relieves the Church of anxiety about risk and change. To do church is to have decided that openness to one another and to God is the human quest to which we were born and in which we are endlessly upheld. Adaptive church leaders know this, even though they are aware of how far they have still to travel in being sufficiently split open by God to become true mediators of trinitarian social practice. Evidence of our slowness to be real, self-aware and open is to be seen, for example, in unwillingness to accept and review situations that failed or to disallow the inclusion of emotional response into the culture of the diocese or parish. Organizational consultants report that in the face of major issues, difficult decisions and possibly an infinite number of potential responses, the general reaction is to remain on safe ground, making minor modifications to the institution but largely maintaining the status quo. Church leaders, with the theology of God's dynamic interwoven in the whole of life, have the challenge and resource to take a much more proactive approach.

Through visioning and story-telling, such leaders will seek to paint a picture of what might be and demonstrate safe ways of achieving change to reach the particular goal. But providing pictures and stories is not, in itself, sufficient to engage a Church that has become reluctant and nervous. The third role of the modern leader is to make it possible for the organization, in all its members, to turn ideas into action. As change agents and servants, leaders provide the nurture, education, spiritual resources and encouragement for everyone to work it out together (Boyett and Boyett, 1998, pp. 33ff).

Change agents in the Church, like prophets, review and challenge the way things are. True prophets of every age, reluctantly, have received their message as a hot burning coal from the altar of deep worship and love for God. Through being personally and politically aware of the deepest meanings to be found in the triune God, prophet leaders will be questioning accepted norms and encouraging individuals and groups to respond with their own visions and solutions. Prophets of the First Testament, through acted symbol, narrative and rhetoric, acted as a mirror to people and communities, challenging behaviour and belief. Their aim was not to destroy existing human structures, but rather to test their continuing validity in the present situation. It is crucial that leaders, in acting prophetically, have a clear understanding of the Church's core values and the skill to connect theology and practice. As Bishop Jamieson has shown, an essential element of the leader's role is to be alert to the risk when core values themselves are being challenged, for the impact of undermining those values in an adaptive organization is to take away its very foundations.

One of the sharp problems in times of rapid change is the need to unlearn things that are no longer helpful or appropriate for the organization. This is a difficult process and one that can cause symptoms of bereavement such as anxiety, defensiveness and resistance to change (Edgar H. Schein in Hesselbein *et al.*, 1996, p. 64).

Schein recognizes the strength and place of the individual people in organizations but argues that while there is a need to continue to develop personal competence, there is also a need for greater and more effective cooperation. He proposes 'cognitive redefinition' as a means of encouraging organizations to move towards effective working between individuals, recognizing and rewarding individuals for good corporate behaviours. The three elements or stages of his concept are (1) a redefinition of what it means to be an individual person, (2) helping individual people to recognize the value of collaborative as well as competitive behaviours, while retaining a sense of individualism, and (3) changing perceptions of competition (within the organization) as being less positive and less welcome than collaboration. His understanding is that attempting to achieve change from an individualistic to a collaborative culture by decree from above has very limited potential. The most potent way requires leaders to demonstrate in themselves and in structural processes the very qualities they seek for the organization. Dioceses and parishes on transformational journeys learn that time, pastoral care, listening, openness and the deliberate inclusion of difference are essential for authentic change.

Implicit within the change agent role is that of servant, especially through helping others to define their own objectives (within the local context and apostolic and catholic values). The servant leader is a primary resource to help others, separately and corporately, to discover and then fulfil their unique calling. Essentially it is not the leader's objectives that are being achieved but more subtly the will of the entire Church, including the leaders, negotiated together under the guidance of the Holy Spirit. Instead of being master builders, servant leaders 'view the organization as a garden and themselves as gardeners' (Boyett and Boyett, 1998, p. 39). The biblical theme of gardens and gardeners brings out thick, textured images both of humanity in the tender but tough hands of the Lord and also of the vocation of humanity as gardener of creation to bring it to its final flowering. Bishops, archdeacons and clergy need to learn how, as change agents in a Church structured to echo the dynamic relationality that is God, to be enablers. In this way the Church can find its total energy as others are nurtured in finding the way for themselves. The great benefit of this approach, despite initial resistance, is the growing sense of the value and varied contribution of each church member in the rhythms of gathering and dispersing to serve God's Kingdom. The life and energy of God is focused only temporarily on the Church in that it truthfully participates in 'the Trinitarian dynamic of holiness in the world' (Hardy, 2001, p. 150).

Leading in truth and holiness

In *Blown to Bits: How the New Economics of Information Transforms Strategy*, Evans and Wurster remind all organizations, including the Church, of the need to consider three dimensions of their life: (1) the depth, richness or intensity of their work, (2) what is their range and reach: with how many different people and groups are they 'in business'? (3) the level of affinity or contact: how far are they really in touch even with those who are committed? The Spirit-filled Church has the task of resourcing deeply all its baptized, worshipping and varied participants in their vocation to exemplify God's blessing, love and holiness for society. To do this effectively the Church, as any other organization, will need to work out its current priorities, ensure the constant cultivation of wisdom in all its members, distribute tasks, help everyone to know their place, expertise and differing responsibilities, to know who is holding everyone together in the Church's purpose and character (episcope, oversight) and to watch out for and listen to those in danger or on the edge. Jesus promised that God's new kingdom begins with 'the least of these'.

One of the recurrent themes of this study has been the recognition of creative ambivalence, the place between utter chaos and linear control. Churches and organizations generally cannot live with total unpredictability. In terms of budget, personnel, or medium-term planning, it is not realistic for a corporation of any kind to be totally open to the future. A vision has to be formed partly according to the intentional core values or meaning of the company and on the basis of reliable knowledge about the environment, finance and levels of employment. Churches share with business and institutions the need to maintain their vulnerability (discover their capacity) for occupying a turbulent but not unpredictable position, somewhere between critical conditions in the heat of the current situation and the certainty of a long-term vision. In multiple contexts in a state of flux, uniform remedies or long-term certainties are unavailable.

The business of doing church is to live publicly and riskily the meanings about God inherent in the gospel of Jesus Christ. So church is the corporate and open practice of the energetic power of the trinitarian God in the world. The Church mediates the purposes of God, especially as an advance sign and a catalyst of all that is contained in God's final hope for creation. Some organizational theorists call this deep meaning the 'information', not as data, but as the social embodiment of their truth or wisdom. Leaders search in ever-new situations for a vision in which the 'glue' is that which connects the rich information with delivery to a wide range of places and people. In this sense the vision is always fluctuating, so as to ensure the linking of the information with delivery points, but in itself it is the constant, binding together everything and everyone.

The power of the Church for its task evaporates when its participants have little affinity with the boundless depth and range of its 'information' which is the true meaning to be found in the dynamics of God's life, inherent in the gospel. Worshipping communities of Christians cannot hope to show the world its true potential until they are prepared to be formed in the truth and wisdom of Christ:

> Because the life and purposes of God are *for the world*, learning the wisdom of Christ is also intrinsically connected to understanding the world and ourselves. That is why, when properly pursued, all forms of learning – from the sciences to social understanding, to language culture and the arts – are ways by which human beings are shaped in the truth and holiness of God. (Hardy, 2001, p. 171)

Previous generations of organizations and church managed, presented and delivered their unique 'information' through proprietary information systems and hierarchic control, vertically integrated value chains, or sequences of linear activities from design to delivery and support of product (Evans and Wurster, 2000). Business analysts note the particular problems that exist for 'incumbents' saddled with legacy assets, distribution systems, bricks and mortar, or core competencies. Experience shows that internal political debates often slow down the task of facing real issues about future development. It is precisely in the destabilization of competitive advantage that advantage can arise, depending on the vision that then evolves. The Church's transformational learning, in order that its own power structures may have anything redemptive to offer externally, lies through absorbing the theology of the necessary and permanent deaths of previous patterns of authority. Church community exists to communicate the truth about the triune God, as free, plastic and beyond the limits of every dogmatic cage or particular form.

The participatory circle of the Church unites the baptized in specific ways (through worship and organization), for specific purposes (to be one, holy, catholic and apostolic), and is sustained by education, ordained ministry and theological research (Hardy, 1996, p. 219). The exact form of this circle will vary enormously through countless new situations as the Church allows itself to be moved by the Spirit to link the deep meanings it knows in the whole of God with the whole life of people in society. Given the restricted capacity of the Church for acting authentically, to aspire to 'holiness' has a bizarre ring. To describe the Church as 'holy' is to maintain faith in its power to indicate how the quality of its being in relatedness, internally and externally, can mirror the quality of the perichoretic relationship between the Persons of the Trinity. As a sign and foretaste of the wholeness that is the holy order destined by God for the entire creation, the Church is invited to be that community which models to all humanity the style of relatedness that most truly echoes the triune being. Through the Spirit, the Church is invited to be a provisional and exploratory example and contemporary identification of God's ultimate hope based in the 'common worth' of all creation (Moltmann, 1989, p. 68)

We have recognized the Church's need to move on urgently from former tendencies to locate its holiness with the clergy, forms of piety or its own internal liturgies and life. Those who are Christians and work in industry or in any 'secular' organization have an exciting responsibility to make connections between faith and work in order to help society as a whole discover better how to live and work together through truthful, shared meanings, in what John Wesley called 'social holiness'. A profound implication of this study is that God intends the whole of the performance of Christian community practice to be infused or inscribed with the whole of God's relational presence, 'a story privileged by faith, the key to the interpretation and regulation of all other stories' (Milbank, 1990, p. 386). Holiness in the Church is not to be equated merely with the attempt to adhere to an alternative moral programme rooted in the teaching of Jesus. Rather, holy relatedness is the 'information', the distilled performance of the Kingdom (David Ford's *habitus*) that is the direct result of the Church, through the exuberant gift of communion in the Trinity, entering into God's saving mission for all creation. The Church, formed by the truth of God's dynamic rule, in the trajectories of its own performance of life in all its fullness is a response to God and an invitation to society.

In contrast with mere ethical programmes, holiness lies more in the direction of the 'being-in-relatedness' that is a response to the enactment in Jesus and the narrative of the community that is inseparable from him, of the dynamic transcendence of the Trinity. The practice of community, founded on the gift of the victory of Christ, a gift constantly made new by the decisive action of the Spirit in baptism and eucharist, is called to show the world how to live in the meaning it finds in God: that is, a model of compassionate and redeemed relationality able to assist in the deconstruction of diminishing and destructive concepts and networks of power. Its vocation, to show the world a model of redeemed relationality, is discovered when children, women and men, inclusively and openly, tenuously begin to communicate with one another in practical ways that are intentionally informed by the sociality of the trinitarian Persons. In the desire for redeemed sociality, the eucharistic assembly is not just a meeting of the faithful. It is the corporate, public, tangible, deep and exhilarating enactment of the meaning of God for all living. It is a sign and foretaste of that community of difference in relation which will be God's fulfilled work. Reflecting on their walk on the road to Emmaus with the stranger who was in fact Jesus, the disciples' 'hearts burned within them' (Luke 24.13–35). This story is evocative of many of the highest aspirations for truly generative work. Leaders are those who can discover and further evoke, in themselves and others, the power which is the quality of interrelatedness we call the triune God.

Conclusion: Making meaning from God for the life of the world

> Human beings are in one and the same activity looking for *and* creating meaning: patterns of order, schemes of communication in which the confusing experience of life in the world to which we belong (and to which we did not choose to belong) is drawn into language, into the ever-extending web of sharing, perception, experience, selfhood itself, that constitutes human being as human. (Williams, 2000, p. 198)

The central concern of this book is the vital necessity of Christian faith in a society that is degrading. When power is generally assumed to be abusive, authority considered diminishing, intimacy feared and discipline politely scorned, the Christian Church must re-find its vocation by reviewing its understanding and application of power, both for itself and the wider community. A necessary starting point has been the reappraisal of the often inadequate language and imagery we choose to attach to God. Conscious recognition of the significant contribution made by church throughout history to notions of power and human and institutional relating is a stimulus to reflect, where appropriate to repent, and to continue to take a responsible place in redrawing the maps for human living together now. We have emphasized the profound possibilities for a revitalized trinitarian understanding of God: not as one alone, but as an open community of difference in relation at the heart of the universe, the same model for sociality revealed in Jesus, by the Spirit. We are deeply concerned when some forms of Christian practice elect to disdain the insights of human disciplines or to treat scriptural texts and church authority as fixed rather than as a fluid and dynamic engagement led and sustained by the Holy Spirit. Something similar is true for the understanding of the human self, not as atomistic and seeking to discover identity internally, but as the creation of the triune God and therefore designed as a deep structure of inter-relatedness. We have explored how radical women theologians are assisting the reimagining of all life as lived in liminality, on the edge, rather than in linear fixity. The embracing of the darkness need not imply an overbalancing but rather a redressing of a previous imbalance towards stability and the dominance of thought over feelings. This has implications for each person but also for the Church and society, in that the self in general, and the Christian self in particular, is always a construct forged on and beyond boundaries, within the *koinonia* or dance of *perichoresis* that the trinitarian God has etched as the watermark in all creation.

The primary argument has been that power does not belong to individuals or groups. Rather power, understood as the relational energy generated and maintained by the triune God, is to be comprehended and entered into as contextual, that is, through radical patterns of mutuality. Christian insights into the truth and meaning to be found in worshipping the mystery of God who is a community of difference indicate the potential for all human living.

The purpose of this study is to encourage the continued exchange between those who have been authorized in many disciplines to make meaning of the world and those who do so from a position of Christian faith and its practice in vibrant eucharistic community.

We have argued that the Church shares with human institutions the possibility of maintaining its character and meeting its goals only when at the same time it is a worked example of human flourishing and a creative contributor to the webs of global connectedness. This is not a bid for Christian ownership of all that is good and worthwhile. Frequently we have returned to the frailty, blindness and inconsistency of the Church. However, we have suggested that the triune God who is creator and sustainer of all invites all human endeavours to avoid binary opposites. A sustained fault occurs when for people, organizations and societies, grandiosity and despair become polarized or when those who are different, rather than being respected are vilified and persecuted. Learning to enjoy difference, to live with ambivalence, and to dare to open ourselves to others rather than merely live behind the masks of our public roles, all signify the potential of living as a deliberate echo of the freedom of trinitarian living. Another strand of this theme is the advocacy of team working in which the equality of roles interplays with the distinctive contribution, personality and uniqueness of each. This book has not been explicitly about ministerial futures for the Church but rather about the shape of the Church's evangelistic openness and responsibility to society. It does, however, naturally invite the reader to use his or her imagination to ask certain questions. Why does the church in my village or town exist? Why does it seem to be in competition with other churches? Why do so few people take notice or even know (let alone understand or believe) its gospel? Why can't it make a better job of being an inviting sign and a compelling reading of all that society now needs in huge measure?

We have been particularly concerned here with the possibilities for living from the holiness of God. Many contemporary books on mission emphasize that we live in a society that loves Jesus, wants to know God, but is bored by church. A deep theme of our work is that in reality the gospel is inherent in the being-in-relatedness that is the public practice of church. We are unable to distinguish between an objective, individualistic discipleship and free action as a participant in the movement that we call church, charged with the ordering of the world according to the meaning we find in God. Respecting and learning from organizational theory seems often to be at the expense of the dynamic foundations of Christian faith. Central now to the Church's evangelistic task is showing society the amazing blessings that become available when we dare to open ourselves individually and corporately to the full relationality of God, and allow that openness to empower all our relationships and organizations. The renewed Spirit-led, catholic Anglicanism implicit in this study does not define itself as against certain people or church decisions. Rather it makes a theologically undergirded attempt to show how the contingent and always experimental practice of the gospel in ever new situations cannot help but desire to be in partnership with all who anticipate and contribute to the world's good end. It is a holistic approach in that it challenges the Church, ecumenically, to work with those in society who are coming to recognize that intellect, feelings and senses need to combine and that each unique person can be respected and welcomed for bringing these in differing measure. In the final chapter we draw some conclusions for the kind of leadership that is urgently required now. Heroic leaders feature well in legends, but the necessary sustainability and humanizing of all purposeful organizations today requires leaders who will hold every participant to a common responsibility for maintaining the internal and external relationships by which the shared character is maintained and the desired outcome achieved.

This volume is an attempt to renew confidence in those who 'belong' to or 'lead' church. Instead of moving too fast to questions about effectiveness with young people, the maintenance of buildings in good order or more relevant worship, we advocate the starting point that, as ultimate authority belongs to the God shown in Jesus, we ask how we can use our precious resources to serve God's mission.

Our ultimate aim has been to fire the imagination so that the untapped energy and potential of people and organizations can be creatively developed. We have also offered a theory of church as a practical example of the dynamics and love of God. This church knows, but is not bound by, its weakness. It appreciates and celebrates the dynamic life of God that it is called to display with ever more confidence and energy. Instead of its energy being leaked and frustrated, it begins to know no bounds and grows in its self-awareness and capacity to reform itself. Its leaders, well aware of their responsibilities and limitations, dare to be so open to the working of God's Spirit within them that their energy and insight are undimmed and their hope for the world grows in response to their perception of need. The Divine Trinity is the source and shape of this church's navigation of new routes, language and integral living for all. The corporate worship of the Trinity, especially in the eucharistic celebration of word and sacrament, is the principal arena for growing into the paradox or ambivalence that is the mature call to become truly human. The Church now, in any given place, is often small in numbers. However, our hope is that this book will have shown that other matters should concern us rather more acutely. As we have seen, there is no following Jesus Christ without many demanding deaths. Our invitation is to be the kind of church that cares little for its own trivial but much-discussed problems and strident disagreements. In fact, if we dare to recognize it, we have good measure, pressed down, shaken together and running over (Luke 6.38). In focusing on God's project for the world's fulfilment, and holding to God's stubborn promise of faithfulness, in partnership with all who have the welfare of the world in their heart, we shall find that we are given all that we could ever need.

Bibliography

Ammicht-Quinn, Regina, Haker, Hille and Junker-Kenny, Maureen, 2004. 'The Structural Betrayal of Trust', *Concilium*, 2004/3.

Archbishops' Council, 2003. *Formation for Ministry within a Learning Church: The Structure and Funding of Ordination Training*, London: Church House Publishing.

Altizer, J. J. (ed.), 1967. *Toward a New Christianity: Readings in the Death of God Theology*, New York: Harcourt, Brace.

Armstrong, Regis, J., 1994. *St Francis of Assisi, Writings for a Gospel Life*, London: St Paul's.

Astley, Jeff (ed.), 2002. *Ordinary Theology: Looking, Listening and Learning in Theology*, Aldershot: Ashgate.

Astley, Neil (ed.), 2003. *Staying Alive: Real Poems for Unreal Times*, London: Bloodaxe.

Ball, Peter, 1988. *Adult Believing: A Guide to the Christian Initiation of Adults*, London: Mowbray.

Barbour, I. G., 1993. *Religion in an Age of Science*, Gifford Lectures 1989–1990, vol. 1, London: SCM.

Barclay, William, [1964] 1998. *The Lord's Prayer*, Berkhamsted: Arthur James.

Barker, H. Gaylon (ed.), 2002. *The Cross at Ground Zero*, Lutheran Reflections and Sermons in Response to 9/11, New York: Metropolitan New York Mission Institute.

Barrow, Simon, 2002. 'Unleashing The Vulnerable Word: Reflections on Ched Myers as a Provocateur for a Healing Church', *British Journal of Theological Education*, vol. 12.2, pp. 95–107.

Barrow, Simon, 2003. 'From Management to Vision', *International Review of Mission*, vol. XCII, no. 364, pp. 7ff.

Bauckham, Richard and Hart, Trevor, 1989. *Hope against Hope: Christian Eschatology in Contemporary Context*, London: Darton, Longman & Todd.

Begbie, Jeremy S., 2000. *Theology, Music and Time: Cambridge Studies in Christian Doctrine*, Cambridge: Cambridge University Press.

Belbin, Meredith, 1996a. *Management Teams: Why they Succeed or Fail*, Oxford: Butterworth-Heinemann.

Belbin, Meredith, 1996b. *Team Roles at Work*. Oxford: Butterworth-Heinemann.

Bennis, Warren, Spreitzer, Gretchen M. and Cummings, Thomas G. (eds), 2001. *The Future of Leadership*, San Francisco: Jossey-Bass.

Biggar, Nigel, 2000, 'Is Stanley Hauerwas Sectarian?' in Nation, Mark Thiessen and Wells, Samuel, *Faithfulness and Fortitude: In Conversation with the Theological Ethics of Stanley Hauerwas*, Edinburgh: T & T Clark.

Blanchard, Ken and Johnson, Spencer, 2004. *The One Minute Manager*, London: Harper-Collins.

Boff, Leonardo, 1988. *Trinity and Society*, Maryknoll: Orbis.

Bohm, David, 1995. *Wholeness and the Implicate Order*, London and New York: Routledge.

Bolman, Lee G. and Deal, Terrence E., 2003a. 'Reframing Ethics and Spirit', in Kouzes, James M. (ed.), *Business Leadership*, San Francisco: John Wiley.

Bolman, Lee G. and Deal, Terrence E., 2003b. 'Reframing Leadership', in Kouzes, James M. (ed.), *Business Leadership*, San Francisco: John Wiley, pp. 86ff.

Bonhoeffer, Dietrich, [1937] 1954. *The Cost of Discipleship*, London: SCM.

Booker, Mike and Ireland, Mark, 2003. *Evangelism – Which Way Now? An Evaluation of Alpha, Emmaus, Cell Church and other Contemporary Strategies for Evangelism*, London: Church House Publishing.

Borgeson, Josephine and Wilson, Lynne (eds), 1990. *Reshaping Ministry: Essays in Memory of Wesley Frensdorff*, Arvada, CO: Jethro Publications.

Boyett, J. and Boyett, J., 1998. *The Guru Guide*, New York: John Wiley.

Bradstock, Andrew and Trotman, Arlington, 2003. *Asylum Voices: Experiences of People Seeking Asylum in the United Kingdom*, London: Churches Commission for Racial Justice, Churches Together in Britain and Ireland.

Brock R. N., 1988. *Journeys by Heart: A Christology of Erotic Power*, New York: Crossroad.

Brown, Raymond, 1984. *The Churches the Apostles Left Behind*, New York: Paulist Press.

Bruce, Steve, 2003. 'The Demise of Christianity in Britain', in Davie, Grace, Heelas, Paul and Woodhead, Linda (eds), 2003. *Predicting Religion. Christian, Secular and Alternative Futures*, Aldershot: Ashgate.

Brueggemann, Walter, 1978. *The Prophetic Imagination*, Minneapolis: Fortress Press.

Brueggemann, Walter, 1997. *Theology of the Old Testament: Testimony, Dispute, Advocacy*, Minneapolis: Fortress Press.

Brueggemann, Walter, 2000. *Texts that Linger, Words that Explode: Listening to Prophetic Voices*, Minneapolis: Fortress Press.

Brueggemann, Walter, 2002. *Ichabod Toward Home: The Journey of God's Glory*, Grand Rapids and Cambridge: Eerdmans.

Brueggemann, Walter, 2003. *Awed to Heaven, Rooted in Earth: Prayers of Walter Brueggemann*, Minneapolis: Fortress Press.

Brueggemann, Walter, 2004. *Inscribing the Text. Sermons and Prayers of Walter Brueggemann*, Minneapolis: Fortress Press.

Burgess, Neil, 2002. *Into Deep Water*, Rattlesden: Kevin Mayhew.

Cammock, Peter, 2003. *The Dance of Leadership: The Call for Soul in 21st Century Leadership*, Auckland: Pearson Education New Zealand.

Capowski, Genevieve, 1994. 'Anatomy of a Leader: Where are the Leaders of Tomorrow?', *Management Review*, March, p. 12.

Childs, James M., Jr, 1995. *Ethics in Business, Faith at Work*, Minneapolis: Fortress Press.

Church, Tara, 2001. 'Where the Leaders Are: The Promise of Youth Leadership' in Bennis Warren, Spreitzer, Gretchen M. and Cummings, Thomas G. (eds), *The Future of Leadership*, San Francisco: Jossey-Bass.

Clark, David, 2004. 'Mission in a "Society without God"', *Crucible*, April–July, pp. 29ff.

Clitherow, Andrew, 2004. *Renewing Faith in Ordained Ministry*, London: SPCK.

Coakley, Sarah, 2002. *Powers and Submissions: Spirituality, Philosophy and Gender*, Oxford: Blackwell.

Collins, John, 1990. *Diakonia: Re-interpreting the Ancient Sources*, New York: Oxford University Press.

Covey, Stephen, 1999. *The Seven Habits of Highly Effective People*, Sydney: Simon & Schuster.

Crafts, Nick, 2004. 'Setting the Scene: an overview of the new economy', in *Spirit at Work*, 1, April.

Daniel, Lilian, 2004. 'Readings in Light of Congregations', *Conversations in Religion and Theology*, vol. 2, no. 2, pp. 240ff.

Davey, Andrew, 2004. Editorial, *Crucible*, July–September, pp. 3ff.

Davie, Grace, 2004. 'Christianity Moving into the Future', *Conversations in Religion and Theology*, vol. 2, no. 2, pp. 217ff.

Dawn, Marva J., 2001. *Powers, Weakness, and the Tabernacling of God*, Grand Rapids and Cambridge: Eerdmans.

Deal, T. and Kennedy, A., 2000. *The New Corporate Cultures*, London: Texere Publishing.

Dear, John, (ed.), 1998. *The Road to Peace*, New York: Orbis.

de Gruchy, John W., 2002. *Reconciliation: Restoring Justice*, London: SCM.

de Mello, Anthony, 1998. *Called to Love: Meditations*, Amand, Gujarat: Gujarat Sahitya Prakash.

Dennis, Trevor, 2004. *God Treads Softly Here*, London: SPCK.

Church of England General Synod, Doctrine Commission, 2003. *Being Human. A Christian understanding of personhood illustrated with reference to power, money, sex and time*, London: Church House Publishing.

Donovan, Vincent, 1982. *Christianity Rediscovered: An Epistle from the Masai*, London: SCM.

Downey, John, K. (ed.), 1999. *Love's Strategy: The Political Theology of Johann Baptist Metz*, Harrisburg, PA: Trinity Press International.

Drane, John, 2000. *The McDonaldization of the Church: Spirituality, Creativity and The Future of the Church*, London: Darton, Longman & Todd.

Drucker, Peter, [1955] 1968. *The Practice of Management*, London: Pan.

Drucker, Peter, [1977] 1979. *Management*, London: Pan.

Drucker, Peter, 2002. 'They're not Employees, They're People', *Harvard Business Review*, February, pp. 70ff.

Dubrin, Andrew, J., 2001. *Leadership, Research Findings, Practice and Skills*, 3rd edition, Boston and New York: Houghton Mifflin.

Dussel, Enrique, 1994. 'Face-to-face with the poor' in Walton, Martin *Marginal Communities: The Ethical Enterprise of the Followers of Jesus*, Kampen: Kok Pharos Publishing House.

Eastman, A. Theodore, 1982. *The Baptizing Community Christian Initiation and the Local Congregation*, New York: Seabury.

Ecclestone, Alan, 1986. *Spirituality and Human Wholeness*, London: British Council of Churches.

Edwardes, Michael, 1983. *Back from the Brink*, London: Collins.

Egenolf, Peter, 2003. 'Vocation and Motivation. The Theories of Luigi Rulla', *The Way*, July, pp. 81ff.

Evans, Philip and Wurster, Thomas S., 2000. *Blown to Bits: How the New Economics of Information Transforms Strategy*, Boston, MA: Harvard Business School Press.

Evely, Louis, trans. Bonin, Edmond, 1965. *That Man is You*, Cork: Mercier Press.

Faber, Alyda, 2004. 'Eros and Violence', *Feminist Theology*, vol. 12.3, May, pp. 319ff.

Ferder, Fran and Heagle, John, 1992. *Your Sexual Self: Pathway to Authentic Intimacy*, Notre Dame, Indiana: Ave Maria Press.

Florence, Anna Carter, (ed.), 2004. *Inscribing the Text: Sermons and Prayers of Walter Brueggemann*, Minneapolis: Fortress Press.

Ford, David F., 1999. *Self and Salvation: Being Transformed*, Cambridge: Cambridge University Press.

Ford, David F. and Stamps, Dennis L., 1996. *Essentials of Christian Community: Essays for Daniel W. Hardy*, Edinburgh: T & T Clark.

Fordham, Frieda, 1972. *An Introduction to Jung's Psychology*, London: Penguin.

Forrester, Duncan B., 2000. *Truthful Action: Explorations in Practical Theology*, Edinburgh: T & T Clark.

Forrester, Duncan, 2001. *On Human Worth*, London: SCM.

Fox, Patricia A., 2001. *God as Communion: John Zizioulas, Elizabeth Johnson, and the Retrieval of the Symbol of the Triune God*, Minnesota: The Liturgical Press.

Galloway, Kathy. 1999. *A Story to Live By*, London: SPCK.

Gill, Robin, 1983. *The Myth of the Empty Church*, London: SPCK.

Gill, Robin, 2003. *The 'Empty' Church Revisited*, Aldershot: Ashgate.

Gill, R. and Burke, D., 1996. *Strategic Church Leadership*, London: SPCK.

Girard, René, 1987. *Things Hidden Since the Foundation of the World*, London: Athlone.

Girard, René, 2001. *I See Satan Fall Like Lightning*, New York: Orbis.

Girard, René, 2003. 'The Mimetic Theory of Religion', in Gifford, Paul (ed.) *2000 Years and Beyond: Faith Identity and the 'Common Era'*, London: Routledge, pp. 88ff.

Goleman, Daniel, 1996. *Emotional Intelligence*, London: Bloomsbury.

Goleman, Daniel, Boyatzis, Richard and McKee, Annie, 2002. *The New Leaders: Transforming the Art of Leadership into the Science of Results*, London: Little, Brown.

Greenwood, Robin, 1999. *Practising Community: The Task of the Local Church*, London: SPCK.

Greenwood, Robin, 2000. *The Ministry Team Handbook: Local Ministry as Partnership*, London: SPCK.

Greenwood, Robin, 2002. *Transforming Church: Liberating Structures for Ministry*, London: SPCK.

Grey, Mary, 1997. *Beyond the Dark Night: A Way Forward for the Church?*, London: Cassell.

Grey, Mary C., 2000. *The Outrageous Pursuit of Hope: Prophetic Dreams for the Twenty-First Century*, London: Darton, Longman & Todd.

Grint, Keith, 1995. *Management: A Sociological Introduction*, Cambridge: Polity Press.

Gunton, Colin, 1998. *The Triune Creator: A Historical and Systematic Study*, Edinburgh: Edinburgh University Press.

Gunton, Colin, 2000. 'Dogmatic Theses on Eschatology' in McFadyen, A., Sarot, M. and Thiselton, A. (eds), *The Future as God's Gift. Explorations in Contemporary Theology*, Edinburgh: T & T Clark.

Gunton, Colin, 2003. *Father, Son and Holy Spirit: Towards a Fully Trinitarian Theology*, London: T & T Clark.

Gunton, Colin and Hardy, Daniel W., 1989. *On Being the Church: Essays on the Christian Community*, Edinburgh: T & T Clark.

Halloran, James, 1996. *Small Christian Communities: A Pastoral Companion*, Dublin: Columba.

Hammarskjöld, Dag, 1964. *Markings*, London: Faber & Faber.

Handy, Charles, [1989] 1990. *The Age of Unreason*, London: Arrow.

Hardwicke, Owen, 2003. *Disciples, Apostles, Ministers*, London: Blackfriars Publications.

Hardy, Daniel W., 1996. *God's Ways with the World: Thinking and Practising Christian Faith*, Edinburgh: T & T Clark.

Hardy, Daniel W., 2001. *Finding the Church*, London: SCM.

Hardy, Daniel W., 2003. 'The Church after September 11: A Study of Social Forms', *International Journal for the Study of the Christian Church*, vol. 3, no. 1.

Hauerwas, Stanley, 1999. *After Christendom? How the Church is to Behave if Freedom, Justice, and a Christian Nation are Bad Ideas*, Nashville, TN: Abingdon.

Hauerwas, Stanley and Spinks, Bryan, 1998. *Sanctify Them in the Truth: Holiness Exemplified*, Edinburgh: T & T Clark.

Harvey, Anthony, 2001. *By What Authority?*, London: SCM.

Headington, Edward W., 2001. 'Seeking a Newer World' in Bennis Warren, Spreitzer, Gretchen M. and Cummings, Thomas G. (eds), *The Future of Leadership*, San Francisco: Jossey-Bass.

Heifetz, Ronald A. and Laurie, Donald, L., 1997. 'The Work of Leadership', *Harvard Business Review on Leadership*, Havard Business School, pp. 171ff.

Herzberg, Frederick, 1968. 'One more time: how do you motivate employees?', *Harvard Business Review*, vol. 46, no. 1, pp. 53–62.

Herzberg, Frederick, 1987. 'Workers' needs the same around the world', *Industry Week*, 21 September, pp. 29–30 and 32.

Hesselbein, F., et al., 1996. *The Leader of the Future*, San Francisco: Jossey-Bass.

Heyward, Isabel Carter, 1982. *The Redemption of God: A Theology of Mutual Relation*, Lanham, MD: University Press of America.

Heyward, Carter, 1989. *Touching our Strength: The Erotic as Power and the Love of God*, San Francisco: Harper & Row.

Huczynski, Andrej and Buchanan, David, 2001. *Organizational Behaviour: An Introductory Text*, 4th edition, London: FT Prentice Hall.

Hughes, Graham, 2003. *Worship as Meaning: A Liturgical Theology for Late Modernity*, Cambridge: Cambridge University Press.

Inge, John, 2003. *A Christian Theology of Place*, Aldershot: Ashgate.

Irigaray, Luce, 2000. *To Be Two*, London: Athlone Press.

Isherwood, Lisa, 2001. 'The Tree, the Cross and Global Capitalism', *Feminist Theology*, no. 28, September.

Isherwood, Lisa, 2004. 'The Embodiment of Feminist Liberation Theology: The Spiralling of Incarnation', in Clack, Beverley, *Embodying Feminist Liberation Theologies*, London: T & T Clark, pp. 140ff.

Jackson, Bob, 2002. *Hope for the Church*, London: Church House Publishing.

Jamieson, Penny, 1997. *Living at the Edge: Sacrament and Solidarity in Leadership*, London: Mowbray.

Jeanrond, Werner G., 1989. 'Community and Authority: The Nature and Implications of the Authority of Christian Community', in Gunton, Colin, *On Being the Church: Essays on the Christian Community*, Edinburgh: T and T Clark.

Jenkins, Timothy, 1999. *Religion in English Everyday Life: An Ethnographical Approach*, New York and Oxford: Berghahn Books.

Jinkins, Michael, 1999. *The Church Faces Death: Ecclesiology in a Post-Modern Context*, Oxford: Oxford University Press.

Johnson, Elizabeth A., 1998. *She Who Is: The Mystery of God in Feminist Theological Discourse*, New York: Crossroad.

Johnson, Elizabeth A., 2003. *Truly our Sister: A Theology of Mary in the Communion of Saints*, New York and London: Continuum.

Johnston, William, 1999. *Being in Love: A Practical Guide to Christian Prayer*, New York: Fordham University Press.

Johnston, William, 2000. *'Arise My Love . . .' Mysticism for a New Era*, Maryknoll: Orbis.

Kagan, Robert, 2003. *Paradise and Power: America and Europe in the New World Order*, London: Atlantic Books.

Keller, Catherine, 2003. *Face of the Deep: A Theology of Becoming*, London: Routledge.

King, Coretta Scott, 1996. *The Words of Martin Luther King, Jr*, New York: Newmarket Press.

Kinlaw, Dennis C., 1995. *The Practice of Empowerment: Making the most of human competence*, Aldershot: Gower.

Kirkpatrick, Damian, Doherty, Philip and O'Flynn, Sheelagh (eds), 2002. *Joy in All Things: A Franciscan Companion*, Norwich: Canterbury Press.

Kleinfield, Annette, 2000. 'Business Identity through Ethical Orientation', *Concilium*, 2000/2, pp. 39ff.

Knight, Douglas, 2000. 'John Zizioulas on the Eschatology of the Person', in Fergusson, David and Sarot, Marcel (eds), *The Future as God's Gift. Explorations in Christian Eschatology*, Edinburgh: T & T Clark.

Kouzes, James M. (ed.), 2003. *Business Leadership*, San Francisco: John Wiley.

Küng, Hans, 1991a. *Theology for the Third Millennium*, London: HarperCollins.

Küng , Hans, 1991b. *Global Responsibility*, New York: Crossroad.

Lazyer, David, 1990. *Cosmogenesis: The Growth of Order in the Universe*, Oxford: Oxford University Press.

Leech, Kenneth, 1977. *Soul Friend. A Study of Spirituality*, London: Sheldon Press.

Leech, Kenneth, 1983. *Spirituality and Pastoral Care*. London: Sheldon Press.

Leech, Kenneth, 1992. *The Eye of the Storm: Spiritual Resources for the Pursuit of Justice*, London: Darton, Longman & Todd.

Levi, Primo, 1958. *If This is a Man*. 1963. *The Truce*. 1979 edition published together, London: Abacus.

Lobinger, Fritz, [1998] 2002. *Like His Brothers and Sisters. Ordaining Community Leaders*, Leominster: Gracewing.

Lynch, Richard, 2003. *Corporate Strategy*, 3rd edition, Harlow: Pearson Education Limited.

Maloney, George, 1994. *That your Joy May Be Complete*, New York: New City Press.

Mantin, Ruth, 2004. 'Theological Reflections on Embodiment', in Clack, Beverley, *Embodying Feminist Liberation Theologies*, London: T & T Clark, pp. 212ff.

Martin, Dale, 1998 in Hauerwas, Stanley and Spinks, Bryan, *Sanctify them in the Truth: Holiness Exemplified*, Edinburgh: T & T Clark.

Martinez, Gaspar, 2001. *Confronting the Mystery of God: Political Liberation and Public Theologies*, London: Continuum.

Maslow, A. H., 1954. *Motivation and Personality*, New York: Harper & Row.

Maslow, A. H., 1971. *The Farther Reaches of Human Nature*, Harmondsworth: Penguin.

McBrien, Richard, 1966. *The Church in the Thought of Bishop John Robinson*, London: SCM.

McFadyen, Alistair I., 1990. *The Call to Personhood: A Christian Theory of the Individual in Social Relationships*, Cambridge: Cambridge University Press.

McFadyen, Alistair, 2000. *Bound to Sin: Abuse, Holocaust and the Christian Doctrine of Sin*, Cambridge: Cambridge University Press.

McGrath, Alister, 2001. *The Future of Christianity*, Oxford: Blackwell.

Metz, J. B., trans. David Smith, 1980. *Faith in History and Society*, New York: Seabury.

Milbank, John, 1990. *Theology and Social Theory: Beyond Secular Reason*, Oxford: Blackwell.

Milbank, John, 2000. *The Word Made Strange*, Oxford: Blackwell.

Miller, Eric, 1993. *From Dependency to Autonomy: Studies in Organizational Change*, London: Free Association Books.

Miller, Keith D., 2004. Review of Charles Marsh, *The Last Days: A Son's Story of Sin and Segregation at the Dawn of a New South*, Conversations in Religion and Theology, pp. 156ff.

Moltmann, Jürgen, 1981. *The Trinity and the Kingdom of God*, London: SCM.

Moltmann, Jürgen, 1989. *Creating a Just Future*, London: SCM.

Moltmann, Jürgen, 2003. 'Progress and Abyss, Remembering the future of the modern world', in Gifford, Paul (ed.), *2000 years and Beyond. Faith, Identity and the 'Common Era'*, London and New York: Routledge, pp. 16ff.

Moltmann, Jürgen, 2003. *The Power of the Powerless*, London: SCM.

Moltmann-Wendel, Elisabeth, 2000. *Rediscovering Friendship*, London: SCM.

Morgan, Gareth, 1997. *Images of Organization*, London: Sage.

Mullan, Dave, 1990. *Ecclesion: The Small Church with a Vision*, Orewa, Aotearoa New Zealand: ColCom Press.

Mullan, Dave and U'ren, David. 2003. *Local Shared Ministry. Strategies for Team Ministry in Small Congregations*, Paihia, Aotearoa New Zealand: ColCom Press.

Myers, Ched, et al., 2000. *'Say to this Mountain', Mark's Story of Discipleship*, Maryknoll, New York: Orbis.

Myerson, George, 2003. *Heidegger, Habermas and the Mobile Phone*, London: Icon Books.

Nanus, Burt, 2003. 'Where Tomorrow Begins: Finding the Right Vision' in Kouzes, James M. (ed.), *Business Leadership*, San Francisco: John Wiley.

Nation, Mark Theissen and Wells, Samuel, 2000. *Faithfulness and Fortitude. In Conversation with the Theological Ethics of Stanley Hauerwas*, Edinburgh: T & T Clark.

Nichols, C. and West, C. 2004. 'Six Shadows', *Innovations*, Berkhamsted: Ashridge Management College.

Nouwen, Henri, 1994. *Here and Now: Living in the Spirit*, New York: Crossroad.

Nouwen, Henri J. M., 2002. *The Wounded Healer*, London: Darton, Longman & Todd.

O'Brien, John, 1994. *Seeds of a New Church*, Dublin: Columba.

Ochs, Peter, 2003. 'Trinity and Judaism', *Concilium*, 2003/4, pp. 51ff.

Ohmae, Kenichi, [1990] 1992. *The Borderless World*, London: Fontana.

Oldham, James, Key, Tony and Starak, Igor Yaro, 1978. *Risking Being Alive*, Bundoora: PIT Publishing.

O'Murchu, Diarmuid, 1997. *Quantum Theology: Spiritual Implications of the New Physics*, New York: Crossroad.

Ortberg, J., 2001. *If You Want to Walk on Water, You've Got to Get Out Of The Boat*, Grand Rapids: Zondervan.

O'Siadhail, Michael, 1992. 'Out of the Blue', in *Hail Madam Jazz*, Newcastle upon Tyne: Bloodaxe Books.

Page, Ruth, 2000. *God with Us: Synergy in the Church*, London: SCM.

Palmer, G. E. H., Sherrard, Philip and Ware, Kallistos, 1979. *The Philokalia. The Complete Text. Vol. 1*, London: Faber & Faber.

Palmer, Parker J., 1998. *The Courage to Teach: Exploring the Inner Landscape of a Teacher's Life*, San Francisco: Jossey-Bass.

Pannenberg, Wolfhart, 1994. *Systematic Theology Vol. 2*, Edinburgh: T & T Clark.

Parkinson, Gary, 2004. 'Stress at work set to spiral for "sandwich generation"', *Daily Telegraph*, 8 April.

Patzia, Arthur G., 2001. *The Emergence of the Church. Context, Growth, Leadership and Worship*, Illinois: InterVarsity Press.

Payne, Claude E. and Beazley, Hamilton, 2001. *Reclaiming the Great Commission: A Practical Model for Transforming Denominations and Congregations*, San Francisco: Jossey-Bass.

Pearce, James, 2000. *Solzhenitsyn – A Soul in Exile*, London: HarperCollins.

Pedler, Mike, Burgoyne, John and Boydell, Tom, 1997. *The Learning Company: A Strategy for Sustainable Development*, 2nd edition, London: McGraw-Hill.

Pennington, M. Basil, 2000. *True Self, False Self: Unmasking the Spirit Within*, New York: Crossroad.

Pennington, M. Basil, 2003. *Call to the Centre: The Gospel's Invitation to Deepest Prayer*, New York: New City Press.

Percy, Martyn, 2003. 'Saving the Roman Catholic Church?', *Conversations in Religion and Theology*, vol. 1, no. 1, pp. 79ff.

Perinbanayagam, R. S., 2000. *The Presence of Self: Taking Leave of Old Concepts and Practices*, Lanham, MD: Rowman and Littlefield.

Perls, Frederick, Hefferline, Ralph F. and Goodman, Paul, 1996. *Gestalt Therapy: Excitement and Growth in the Human Personality*, 2nd edition, London: Souvenir Press.

Perri, William D., 2003. *A Radical Challenge for Priesthood Today, From Trial to Transformation*, Mystic, CT: Twenty Third Publications.

Peters, Tom, 1988. *Thriving on Chaos*, London: Macmillan.

Peters, Tom, 1992. *Liberation Management*, London: Macmillan.

Peters, Tom, 1995. *The Pursuit of Wow! Every Person's Guide to Topsy Turvey Times*, London: Macmillan.

Pettifer, Bryan, G. E., 2002. *Management and Spiritual Energy*, London: MODEM.

Polkinghorne, John, 2003. 'Physics and Metaphysics in a Trinitarian Perspective', *Theology and Science*, vol. 1, no. 1, pp. 33ff.

Prigogine, Ilya and Stengers, Isabelle, 1984. *Order out of Chaos: Man's New Dialogue with Nature*, London: Heinemann.

Rahner, Karl, 1987. *Foundations of Christian Faith: An Introduction to the Idea of Christianity*, New York: Crossroad.

178   *Bibliography*

Rasmusson, Arne, 1994. *The Church as Polis: From Political Theology to Theological Politics as exemplified by Jurgen Moltmann and Stanley Hauerwas*, Studia Theologica Lundensia 49, Lund: Lund University Press.

Richter, Philip and Francis, Leslie, 1998. *Gone but not Forgotten*, London: Darton, Longman & Todd.

Ricoeur, Paul, 1992. *Oneself as Another*, London: University of Chicago Press.

Robertson, James, 1998. *Transforming Economic Life*, London: Green Books.

Rohr, Richard and Martos, Joseph, 1996. *The Wild Man's Journey: Reflections on Male Spirituality*, Cincinnati: St Anthony Messenger Press.

Rulla, Luigi M., 1986 and 1989. *Anthropology of the Christian Vocation*, vols 1 and 2, Rome: Gregorian University Press.

Rural Ministry Publications, 2000. *Country Conversations. The Trans-Tasman Rural Ministry Conference, Northland, 2000*, Paihia, Aotearoa New Zealand: ColCom Press.

Rural Ministry Conference, 2003. 'Reflections from Western Australia', in *Ruminations*, Dubbo, New South Wales: NSW Rural Ministry Unit.

Saris, Wim, 1980. *Towards a Living Church: Family and Community Catechesis*, London: Collins.

Schein, Edgar H., 1996. 'Leadership and Organizational Culture', in Hesselbein, F., et al., *The Leader of the Future*, San Francisco: Jossey-Bass.

Schemann, Alexander, 2002. *For the Life of the World, Sacraments and Orthodoxy*, New York: SVS Press.

Schillebeeckx, Edward, 1980. *Ministry: A Case for Change*, London: SCM.

Schillebeeckx, Edward, 1985. *The Church with a Human Face: A New and Expanded Theology of Ministry*, London: SCM.

Schlier, Heinrich, 1961. *Principalities and Powers in the New Testament*, Edinburgh and London: Nelson.

Searcy, Edwin (ed.), 2003. *Awed to Heaven: Prayers of Walter Brueggemann*, Minneapolis: Fortress Press.

Sedmak, Clemens, 2002. *Doing Local Theology: A Guide for Artisans of a New Humanity*, Maryknoll: Orbis.

Sedgwick, Peter, 1996. 'On Anglican Polity' in Ford, David F., and Stamps, Dennis L. *Essentials of Christian Ministry: Essays for Daniel W. Hardy,* Edinburgh: T & T Clark.

Sedgwick, Peter, 2004. 'A theological response to the new economy', *Spirit in Work*, 1, April.

Senge, Peter, 1990. *The Fifth Discipline: The Art and Practice of the Learning Organization*, New York: Doubleday Currency.

Senge, Peter et al., 1999. *The Dance of Change: The Challenges of Sustaining Momentum in Learning Organizations*, London: Nicholas Brealey.

Sizoo, Lysanne, 2004. 'When the cell doors close and hearts open', *The Way*, October, pp. 161ff.

Solle, Dorothee, (1990) 1991. *Thinking about God. An Introduction to Theology*, London: SCM; Philadelphia: Trinity Press International.

Sorcher, Melvin and Brant, James, 2002. 'Are You Picking the Right Leaders?', *Harvard Business Review*, February, pp. 78ff.

Spalding, Anne, 2001. '"Right Relation" Revisited: Implications of Right Relation in the Practice of Church and Christian Perceptions of God', *Feminist Theology*, no. 28, September, pp. 57ff.

'Statement of the International Contemporary Reflection on Global Oppressed Communities: A Multi-Faith Approach', *Ministerial Formation*, Geneva: WCC.

Storrs, Elizabeth, 2004. '"Our Scapegoat": An Exploration of Media Representations of Myra Hindley and Rosemary West', *Theology and Sexuality*, vol. 11.1.

Stuart, Elizabeth, 2003. *Gay and Lesbian Theologies: Repetitions with Critical Difference*, Aldershot: Ashgate.

Sugirtharajah, R. S., 2003. *Postcolonial Reconfigurations: An Alternative Way of Reading the Bible and Doing Theology*, London: SCM.

Swinney, Frank, 2000. 'Mutual Ministry in Holy Trinity Church, Winton', in *Stories of Anglican Ministry Enabling New Directions*, New Zealand: Diocese of Christchurch.

Tamayo-Acosta, Juan Jose, 2003. 'Dignity and Liberation: A Theological and political Perspective', *Concilium*, 2003/2, pp. 67ff.

Tanner, Kathryn, 1997. *Theories of Culture: A New Agenda for Theology*, Minneapolis: Fortress Press.

Tatman, Lucy, 2004. 'Theological Matricide, Essentially', *Feminist Theology*, vol. 12.3.

Taylder, Sian, 2002. 'The Hour is Coming, the Hour is Come: Church and Feminist Theology in Post-Revolutionary El Salvador', *Feminist Theology*, vol. 11.1.

Taylor F. W., 1915. *The Principles of Scientific Management*, New York: Harper & Brothers.

Thiselton, Anthony C., 2003. 'Conclusion', in Gifford, Paul (ed.), *2000 years and Beyond: Faith, Identity and the 'Common Era'*, London: Routledge, pp. 147ff.

Thomas, R. S., 1995. *Collected Poems 1945–1990*, London: J M Dent.

Tomka, Miklos, 2004. 'Post-Communist Europe and the Continued Existence of Atheism', *Concilium*, 2004/2, pp. 105ff.

Tutu, Desmond, 1999. *No Future without Forgiveness*, London: Rider.

Vanier, Jean, 1999. *Becoming Human*, London: Darton, Longman & Todd.

Vanhoozer, Kevin (ed.), 2003. *The Cambridge Companion to Post-modern Theology*, Cambridge: Cambridge University Press.

Ulrich, Hans G., 2000. 'Being and Becoming a Self in an Ethical Perspective', *Concilium*, 2000/3, pp. 121ff.

Walker, Michael, 1986. *Spirituality and Human Wholeness*, London: WCC.

Wallis, Ian, 2000. *Holy Saturday Faith: Rediscovering the Legacy of Jesus*, London: SPCK.

Walton, Martin, 1994. *Marginal Communities: The Ethical Enterprise of the Followers of Jesus*, Kampen: Kok Pharos Publishing House.

Ward, Hannah and Wild, Jennifer, 1995. *Guard the Chaos. Finding Meaning in Changes*, London: Darton, Longman & Todd.

Ward, Pete, 2002. *Liquid Church*, Peabody, MA: Hendickson.

Warren, Yvonne, 2002. *The Cracked Pot: The State of Today's Anglican Clergy*, London: Kevin Mayhew.

Watson, David, 1978. *I Believe in the Church*, London: Hodder & Stoughton.

Watson, Francis, 2004. 'Deconstructing the Hero', unpublished paper, Society for the Study of Theology meeting at Exeter.

Webster, Alison, 2002. *Society and Church*, London: SCM.

Webster, John, 2003. 'The human person', in Vanhoozer, Kevin J. (ed.), *The Cambridge Companion to Post-modern Theology*, Cambridge: Cambridge University Press.

Williams, Rowan, 2000. *On Christian Theology*, Oxford: Blackwell.

Williamson, Marianne, 1992. *A Return to Love: Reflections on the Principles of A Course in Miracles*, London: HarperCollins.

Young, Frances, 1997. *Encounter with Mystery: Reflections on L'Arche and Living with Disability*, London: Darton, Longman & Todd.

Zaleznik, Abraham, 1998. 'Managers and Leaders: Are They Different?', in Mintzberg, Henry, et al., *Harvard Business Review on Leadership*, Boston, MA: Harvard Business School Press.

Zizioulas, John D., 1985. *Being as Communion: Studies in Personhood and the Church*, New York: St Vladimir's Seminary Press.

Index